C000314208

When Did BIG BEN First Bong?

When Did BIG BEN First Bong?

101 questions answered about the greatest city on Earth

DAVID LONG

Also by David Long

Spectacular Vernacular: London's 100 Most Extraordinary Buildings

Tunnels, Towers & Temples: London's 100 Strangest Places

The Little Book of London

The Little Book of the London Underground

First published 2010

The History Press
The Mill, Brimscombe Port
Stroud, Gloucestershire, GL5 2QG
www.thehistorypress.co.uk

British Library Cataloguing in Publication Data.
A catalogue record for this book is available from the British Library.

ISBN 978 0 7524 5584 6

Typesetting and origination by The History Press
Printed in Great Britain

CONTENTS

'I still love London, no matter what they do to it.'
– Sir Michael Caine CBE

1

ART & ARCHITECTURE

What is the **earliest** known **image** of London?

It appears on the reverse of the fourth-century, gold 'Arras Medallion', a replica of which is in the British Museum.

In AD 286 one Marcus Aurelius Mausaeus Carausius, a successful Roman military commander who had been appointed provincial governor, rebelled against his masters and declared himself to be the new emperor of Roman Britain and Northern Gaul. Under the circumstances his reign proved surprisingly enduring, lasting for seven years before he was murdered by his treasurer Allectus. The former finance minister in turn announced that he was now emperor, and even commenced construction of a magnificent Imperial palace close to St Peter's Alley, Cornhill, although work on this stopped when he was himself eventually overcome.

The restoration to legitimate Roman rule came in 296 when the loyal general Constantius Chlorus arrived in Britain to find Londinium being sacked by gangs of Frankish mercenaries in the pay of Allectus. Determined to call a halt to this, he had a flotilla of Roman warships known as the *Classis Britannica* sail up the Thames. Upon reaching their destination – to quote the words of a later panegyric to Constantius – the force 'found the survivors of the barbarian mercenaries plundering the city, and, when these began to seek flight, [the Romans] landed and slew them in the street. Not only did they bring safety to your subjects by the timely destruction of the enemy, but, also induced a sentiment of gratitude and pleasure at the sight.'

The attractive nine *solidi* medallion was struck to commemorate this momentous event, showing Constantius Chlorus on one side accepting acclaim as *REDDITOR LVCIS AETERNAE*, the Restorer of Eternal Light. On the reverse a woman representing the spirit of London is seen kneeling at the Roman city wall welcoming a mounted Roman soldier and thanking him for terminating the rule of Allectus. Despite the object's relevance locally, the name derives from its discovery in the French town of Arras in September 1922, with the medallion thought to have been minted in about AD 310 in Trier on the Moselle river, one of the oldest cities in modern Germany.

Where is **London's longest tunnel**?

Somewhat incredibly, until 1988 a branch of the Northern Line was the longest railway tunnel in the world with the route from East Finchley to Morden via Bank running for 17 miles and 528 yards to serve no fewer than twenty-four stations. However, today it is not even longest tunnel in London as this record belongs to another subterranean network altogether; one which runs far deeper underground than the Tube ever did, which extends considerably further than the Channel Tunnel, and yet which these days is used for nothing more than transporting tap water around the capital.

If that makes the Thames Water Ring Main sound like a mere pipe, however, this is a misconception which needs correcting straight away. For one thing, it is truly enormous: 50 miles all the way round, at least, and still being added to with many miles of extensions being planned as far ahead as 2025. It took years to build as well, with work on the first stage alone taking from 1988 until the summer of 1994. And so far it's cost us around a quarter of a billion smackers which is way more than most of us would stump up to sink a little ducting.

It's also as fat as a proper tunnel, the diameter of 8ft 4in putting it close to that of, say, the Greenwich Foot Tunnel or Tower Subway and meaning it's plenty big enough to run trains through. Indeed during much of its construction it was fitted out with a bespoke narrow-gauge railway to ferry workmen and tools around, as well as later being used as the venue for a charity bicycle race once the tracks had been taken up and the trains towed away.

Perhaps because it's lost to public view – above ground the most visible part is Damian O'Sullivan and Tania Doufa's thrilling, RIBA award-winning tower on Holland Park roundabout – most Londoners don't know it's down there and of those who do, one suspects, hardly anyone stops to consider what a triumph of engineering it is. Did the project overrun? No idea. Was it over budget when they had finished? Who cares! Instead, now the bulk of it is completed, it's a wonder to behold, constructed on the scale of Sir Joseph Bazalgette's famous sewers (albeit without quite the same aesthetic finesse) and able to pump clean water from the Thames and Lea river systems around Greater London at a sufficient lick – 300,000,000 gallons a day – to fill an 50m Olympic swimming pool in just over 25 minutes or, so they say, the Royal Albert Hall to the rafters in only three hours.

It's also a technical tour de force. Hailed as the most sophisticated water-control system of any major world city when it was opened by Her Majesty in November 2004, its £3.2 million Hampton control HQ in south-west London is able, remotely, to continuously monitor water pressures, flows, reservoir levels and even quality for millions of homes and businesses across the entire spread of Greater London. Hitherto this had taken a dozen different centres, none of which could communicate with any of the others, and required miles and miles of bespoke fibre optic cable from Norway – apparently the ordinary stuff rots in normal drinking water – in order to transmit gigabytes of data every day between Hampton and a network of eleven pumping stations which raise the water up from 130ft below to the local pipe network.

The same cabling collects information about the water pressure and quality and can even carry closed-circuit television pictures from the network's security cameras, a uniquely high level of monitoring being vital because the water moves through the main – it can go either way – using gravity rather than external pumps. This requires the tunnels to be full of water at all times, meaning the operators have to know exactly how much water is being used minute-by-minute by Thames Water's seven million customers – and to know precisely how to react when yet another piece of rusty old Victorian pipework fractures to flood the road and throw everything out of kilter.

When did **Big Ben** first **bong**?

Big Ben's first bong rang out across Westminster on 11 July 1859, an occasion marked exactly 150 years later when, at 10 p.m. on the same day in 2009, a special light show commemorating the great bell's birthday was projected onto the south side of the 315ft-high St Stephen's Tower.

There had been a clock tower on the site since about 1288, but the present edifice in Augustus Pugin's ebullient, largely self-invented Gothic Revival style – he had earlier produced something similar for a Lancashire baronet at Scarisbrick Hall – formed part of Charles Barry's design for a new legislative building following the near-total destruction by fire of the old Palace of Westminster on the night of 22 October 1834.

Pugin claimed never to have 'worked so hard in my life for Mr Barry for tomorrow I render all the designs for finishing his bell tower and it is beautiful' – and shortly after completing the project he subsided into madness, collapsed and died at just 40 years of age.

Barry's end of things was technically hugely advanced for its day, the cast iron, brick and limestone-clad tower standing on an immense raft of concrete almost 10ft thick. It has, even so, subsided slightly over the years so that today, with the Jubilee Line Extension tunnellers in no small part responsible for the shift, the tower leans slightly to the north-west. Indeed, at clock face level, it is now nearly 9in off true.

Equivalent to a sixteen-storey building, St Stephen's has long been one of the world's most famous buildings, and is instantly recognisable as perhaps the single most important icon of London. This remains so even though it is not easy for the general public to visit – with no lift it takes a hike up 334 steps for the lucky few to reach the summit – and most people, Londoners and visitors alike, continue to get its name wrong.

Why the Great Bell's nickname should so consistently be applied to the tower remains a complete mystery, as indeed does the origins of the name Ben, especially given the rarity with which most bells – even jolly big ones like this – are accorded nicknames. It could be named after Ben Caunt, a noted bare-knuckle boxer and sometime English Heavyweight Champion, or more probably the noted civil engineer Lord Llanover (otherwise Sir Benjamin Hall Bt) who oversaw its construction in his role as First Commissioner of Works.

Either way the item in question was indeed a very big bell, the first such being a 16-ton monster which was cast on in August 1856 at Stockton-on-Tees and transported to the tower on a trolley drawn by sixteen horses. Unfortunately this one cracked beyond repair before it was even rung officially and a 13½-ton replacement was commissioned from the Whitechapel Bell Foundry (q.v.) in the East End. When completed it was winched 200ft up to the belfry, a feat which took more than 18 hours, but this one also cracked under the hammer, barely two months after that all-important first bong. A repair was effected – during which time it was out of commission for an incredible three full years – but even now the effect of the crack can still be heard in its distinctive and much-loved tone. No-one seems to mind, however, nor for that matter do they care that London's most famously big bell was quickly overtaken, in 1881, by the 16¾-ton 'Great Paul' which was hoisted above the cathedral of that name and hangs there still.

Which is London's **largest square**?

Ask most Londoners and the chances are they'll tell you the answer is Trafalgar – although, paradoxically, this same square is also popularly supposed to cover exactly 1 acre when the actual measure is closer to 5. In fact the largest public square in the capital is some way distant: Lincoln's Inn Fields, at 12 acres, an area dwarfed by the likes of Tiananmen (which is more than 15 times the size) or even the Place de la Concorde in Paris.

It is still a substantial enough spread if you go and take a look, however, and said to have been the inspiration behind New York's Central Park, the design for its layout came from Inigo Jones in the seventeenth century. Unlike Trafalgar Square, however, which was public from the start, the masses had to wait until the end of the nineteenth century to be admitted to Lincoln's Inn Fields when the square was acquired by the

London County Council. The previous owners had been the Honourable Society of Lincoln's Inn, one of the four great Inns of Court, whose students had hitherto had the run of two areas of wasteland called the Purse Field and the Cup Field. With their ownership dating back to the fourteenth century, such scholars who walked and talked here before the public moved in in 1895 would have included many famous names including those of Oliver Cromwell, Sir Thomas More and no fewer than seven future Prime Ministers.

Of these only one warrants a plaque overlooking the park, and that is poor old Spencer Perceval (1762–1812) – the only British Prime Minister to have been assassinated. Shot dead by a berserk merchant broker from Liverpool, actually within the walls of the Palace of Westminster, his murder was foreseen nine days earlier by John Williams of Redruth (in a dream full of vivid detail) but the Cornishman's family dissuaded him from journeying to London to warn the authorities and disaster ensued.

Peaceful now, despite the proximity of noisy High Holborn, it is hard to believe this is the place where tens of thousands gathered to witness the grisly execution of fourteen Catholic traitors in the 1580s. Sentenced to be hanged, drawn and quartered for a plot against Good Queen Bess, contemporary accounts say that the plotters' leader, Sir Anthony Babington, was still alive and aware when his agonising evisceration began.

By contrast London's smallest square is away to the West, buried away in smart St James's. Accessed via a narrow eighteenth-century oak-panelled tunnel squeezed between two of London's oldest and most picturesque shop fronts – and covering just a few square metres – the worn flagstones of Pickering Place are popularly held to have witnessed the last duel ever fought in England. Proving such a claim is never easy – whatever the outcome these things were rarely advertised attractions – but its seclusion would certainly have suited a little illegal sword – or pistol – play, while its proximity to

White's, Arthur's, Brooks's and Boodle's would have made it a most convenient place for the disgruntled gamblers and young blades of London clubland to settle a few personal scores.

Where is the **Great Pyramid** of London?

The short answer is that it never got built, or perhaps that should be *they* never got built since – strange but true – more than once someone, somewhere has proposed building something akin to Cheops right here in the capital.

In 1815, for example, flushed with pride at the defeat on land and on water of the dastardly Bonaparte – and with the fashionable new style of the Nile riding high after a successful Egyptian campaign – a certain Colonel (later Major-General) Sir F.W. Trench MP conceived a plan for a giant pyramid on what is now Trafalgar Square. Large enough to cover virtually the entire square, and at 364ft high, considerably taller than the dome of St Paul's, Sir Frederick estimated that his vast, stepped ziggurat – 22 storeys high, with one tier for each year of the war – would cost a cool £1,000,000, a sum he felt was unlikely to be 'burthensome to the nation'.

Parliament happily disagreed and the scheme got no further, but then in 1829 up popped another one. This time it was to be even larger – considerably larger, in fact, capable of dwarfing even the Great Pyramid itself – with its promoter Thomas Willson declaring his intention to erect on Primrose Hill a pyramid-shaped mausoleum large enough to hold 5,167,104 of London's loved ones.

Trench is these days dismissed as almost the patron saint of architectural lost causes – besides wishing to build over Hyde Park he proposed defiling the river view with a wooden overhead railway – but Willson was far from a crank. The winner of the Royal Academy Schools Gold Medal, his pyramid was nothing if not well thought out with 215,296 catacombs – each large enough to take two dozen dead – an internal chapel for mourners, and accommodation for a keeper, his clerk, a sexton and a superintendent.

Designed with four separate entrances, one on each side, a central ventilation shaft and ramps instead of stairs to facilitate the easy transportation of coffins around what inside looked not unlike a beehive, Willson further promised to provide exceptionally hygienic surroundings with 'every deposit hermetically sealed for ever' in place of London's traditionally pestilential churchyards and plague pits. Also, he said, his scheme would 'beguile the hours of the curious and impress feelings of solemn awe and admiration upon every beholder.'

His trump card, though, was as much financial as aesthetic. With the catacombs rented out at £50 a vault, and 40,000 'customers' a year, Willson estimated that London as a whole would save £12,500 annually against the cost of conventional burial; investors in his Five Per Cent Pyramid Stock would meanwhile see an eventual return of £10,764,800. It sounded too good to be true, and so indeed it was to prove, with the purchase of 54 acres at Kensal Green by the rival General Cemetery Company quickly dishing his plans before the first brick had even been laid.

For pyramids, however, it was not quite all over and in 1903 Dr David Walsh reopened the old argument by calling for a smaller (but uglier) pyramid to be sited atop a hefty plinth 'say, in Hyde Park' with large sloping windows to admit light, a sort of druids' temple at its core, and the planned reburial within of various long-dead kings and queens of England to get the place off to a good start. The public, said Walsh, would be invited to contribute according to their means, with the poor paying for just one or two bricks while the rich would be expected to cough up for a hundred thousand or even a million. The invitation, thank heavens, was declined almost universally so that today the most prominent pyramid in London is Hawksmoor's strangely elongated one on top of St George the Martyr, Bloomsbury. Modelled on the tomb of King Mausolus at Halicarnassus – the original 'mausoleum', and one of the original Seven Wonders of the World – it is indeed so strange that when you get there you'll wonder how you've never noticed it before.

Where is London's **oldest church**?

In Queen Victoria Street in the City the relocated Roman Temple of Mithras dates back to the third century. Early records relating to the foundation of St Paul's Cathedral by Mellitus suggest a date of AD 604. The Church of All Hallows by the Tower contains a Saxon arch built of Roman bricks, and a charter of AD 951 mentions the church of St Andrew's, Holborn, although the present edifice – being by Wren – is clearly not that old.

Instead most historians agree, after leaving aside such fragments and pagan relics as these (and the austere but elegant Chapel of St John in the Normans' White Tower) that the oldest actual church in the capital is St Bartholomew-the-Great in Smithfield. Constructed between 1123 and 1145 – and so predating the equally beguiling Temple Church by a good four decades or more – it includes traces of what are almost certainly the earliest pointed arches in London although today the visitor is more likely to identify the characteristic round-headed arches favoured by Norman builders atop the tremendous, sturdy circular pillars which support the choir.

A surviving piece of the great Augustinian Priory of St Bartholomew, it was founded by Rahere, a worldly courtier and favourite of King Henry I who made a pilgrimage to Rome. Falling ill en route he vowed that were he lucky enough to survive he would establish a hospital for the poor, and travelling home claimed to have seen a vision of the Apostle St Bartholomew who told him what to build and where. Back in England, and miraculously restored to health, Rahere established a new priory of Augustinian canons near Smithfield as well as the adjacent hospital – which we now know as Bart's – with himself serving as both prior and master. Rahere was eventually buried here too, in 1145, although in 1539 the priory was dissolved on the orders of Henry VIII and his great nave demolished.

Perhaps because of its central location most of the monastic buildings were fortunately left intact and put to new uses, with the canons' choir and sanctuary set aside for normal parish duties with a brief spell (under Queen Mary) as a house of Dominican friars. Today, too, it is very much a working church, and a well-known one not least as a consequence of it having provided locations for a number of film and TV crews responsible for, among others, *Shakespeare in Love*, *Four Weddings and a Funeral*, *The Other Boleyn Girl* and (less obviously) *Robin Hood Prince of Thieves*.

How many **towers** make up the **Tower** of **London**?

1. The Beauchamp Tower: named after a fourteenth-century prisoner, Thomas Beauchamp, Earl of Warwick, although today perhaps the most celebrated person to have been

incarcerated within its walls is England's tragic nine-day-queen. While she was still a teenager, Lady Jane Grey's husband carved the word 'Jane' into the wall before the two were led away to their execution.

2. The Bell Tower: dating back to the 1190s, and thus one of the oldest towers, the name refers to a curfew bell which was rung here nightly for more than 500 years. Queen Elizabeth and Sir Thomas More both spent time locked in this tower.

3. The Bloody Tower: originally the Garden Tower but renamed after the legend of the 'Princes in the Tower' took hold suggesting that it was here that their uncle had the pair despatched.

4. The Bowyer Tower: presumably being drowned in a butt of malmsey wine is no better than any other kind of drowning (see the Great London Beer Flood, p. 74) but according to tradition the Bowyer Tower is where Richard III's brother, the Duke of Clarence, met his fate in this singularly memorable fashion.

5. The Brick Tower: Sir Walter Raleigh impregnated one of Elizabeth I's maids of honour but despite doing the honourable thing and marrying her, he incurred the wrath of his sovereign and in 1592 spent some time locked up here before being released and disgraced.

6. The Broad Arrow Tower: a thirteenth-century addition, the name has nothing to do with armaments or defence but refers to a motif applied to Crown property lest anyone wonder who owned the goods which were stored within.

7. The Byward Tower: literally by-warden, referring to its proximity to the Warder's Hall, this being the tower from which the senior warder emerges to secure the premises following the celebrated Ceremony of the Keys each evening.

8. The Constable Tower: traditionally the home of the Constable of the Tower, an ancient and honourable office whose holders were – and in all likelihood still are – entitled to any animal which falls off London Bridge, any carts falling into the moat, a shilling from any boat passing upstream if it is carrying herring, and direct personal access to the Sovereign Head of State.

9. The Cradle Tower: nothing to do with babies, but a reference to a hoist once used to raise up boats from the river.

10. The Develin Tower: a postern gate, and the most easterly tower, this was built by Edward I and formerly led onto a causeway across the moat.

11. The Devereux Tower: named for Robert Devereux, Earl of Essex, a favourite of Elizabeth I's until he attempted to mount a coup in 1601. Locked up here, he was later executed on Tower Hill.

12. The Flint Tower: simple really – it was built of flint during the reign of Henry III although it was substantially altered in Victorian times.

13. The Lanthorn Tower: the name refers to a lantern lit at the top and intended to guide shipping safely up the River Thames.

14. The Lion Tower: demolished in the 1850s, this stood where the ticket office now is and was home to the Royal Menagerie for several centuries until the animals were relocated to the new zoo in Regent's Park.

15. The Martin Tower: otherwise known as the Jewel Tower because from 1669 until the 1840s the Crown Jewels were kept here with at least one serious attempt being made to steal them in 1671 (see p. 70).

16. The Middle Tower: the main entrance for the general public, the name indicates its location between the Lion and Byward towers.

17. St Thomas's Tower: built between 1275 and 1279 by Edward I to provide additional royal accommodation for the king. The name is derived from that of Sir Thomas a Becket who served a term as Constable in the 1160s, and its most famous incumbent is probably the traitor Sir Roger Casement (see p. 66).

18. The Salt Tower: initially Julius Caesar's Tower (and later Balliol's Tower, having once imprisoned John Balliol, King of Scotland) the name probably refers to a period when it was used as secure storage for this valuable commodity. Complex graffiti and carvings bear witness to it having also been, like so many other towers, a prison.

19. The Wakefield Tower: traditionally the tower where Henry VI was murdered while at prayer, the seemingly timeless tradition of laying lilies on the spot where he died was in reality instituted as recently as 1923 with the florist's bill being picked up by Eton College in honour of its royal founder.

20. The Wardrobe Tower: as the name suggests, the tower with its Roman foundations would have been used to store the king's clothing and armour when what remains a royal palace was also a royal residence.

21. The Well Tower: built for King Edward I between 1275 and 1279 by Master James of St George. Besides protecting the palace's river frontage, the tower contained two deep well-shafts through which fresh water could be drawn when or if the occupants came under siege.

22. The White Tower: The Big One. The original and oldest part of the Conqueror's fortress, the name derives from the earliest days when the already imposing structure was whitewashed to further emphasise its dominance over the walled city and the invaders' position over the country as a whole. It's also famous for having the first actual fireplace in England, though without a chimney.

Where is London's **most expensive** private **house**?

For years the answer would have been Kensingston Palace Gardens, a street few Londoners actually know as it is gated and by no means easy to access. It has long been described as the world's most expensive street and on successive occasions sales here have smashed existing records with price tags of £30m, £50m and eventually as much as £70m for one or other of its generous freeholds. It is here, too, that one owner recently lodged a planning application to dig more than 50ft down in order to create not just a full-size, LTA-approved underground tennis court for his family, but also a display area for a collection of historic Ferraris.

In 2009, however, Belgravia struck back in a big way with the *Sunday Times* reporting the capital's first ever triple-figure asking price when one vendor began chasing £100 million for a house in the Duke of Westminster's landmark, stucco-fronted Belgrave Square. At 21,000sq ft with six storeys, 20ft ceilings and a spacious mews at the bottom of the garden, no. 10 was clearly a lot of house, but at that price many self-styled property experts were wondering whether there was anyone out there who would actually pay for it.

Once home to the French Ambassador, and until 1978 the club house of the Institute of Directors, no. 10 Belgrave Square was designed by George Basevi, a cousin of Disraeli's who died after falling from the top of Ely Cathedral. The vendor this time was Musa Salem, a Lebanese developer, who was said to have remodelled the house along similar lines to his own (slightly smaller) house in another famous billionaires' row, namely North London's reliably garish Bishops Avenue. It could be argued, however, that the price, while high, wasn't that outrageous for the area. At the time of writing another house opposite Salem's was also on the market – for a mere £80 million, but then it is only 20,000sq ft – while yet another in the square was for sale at £32 million even though it had less than twenty years remaining on the lease.

With neighbours including the Russian oligarch Oleg Deripaska, Sheikh Mohammed bin Rashid Al Maktoum of Dubai and a number of embassies, you can also be sure that Salem's is a lot of house for the money. The selling agents weren't exactly issuing invitations to come over and check this out, but such houses as these are more than just homes and these days many come equipped with the fullest possible complement of vast indoor pools, underground sports complexes and cinemas, even subterranean mini-multi-storeys for their owners' fleets of Bentleys, Bugattis and Rolls-Royces. One mews house round the corner behind Grosvenor Square, for example, even has a 30ft waterfall in the basement.

What was so **great** about the **Great Fire** of London?

It's a fair question given that London has been burned down so many times over the last twenty centuries. Boudicca famously torched what was at the time a locally important Roman trading post in AD 61, the charred remains of which are still to be encountered when new foundations are dug around the Square Mile. The first, Saxon cathedral to St Paul fell to the flames in 961 and then again in 1087. In the late twelfth century William FitzStephen, a witness to Thomas a Becket's murder, wrote at length describing the twin plagues of London as 'the immoderate drinking of fools and the frequency of fires.' And when both ends of London Bridge went up in 1212–13 as many as 3,000 are thought to have perished in the flames.

But all these – and indeed that other Great Fire near London Bridge in 1861 which killed the capital's fire chief and smouldered from June 'til December – were dwarfed by *the* Great Fire which broke out a little after 1 a.m. on 2 September 1666 and made the name of Pudding Lane famous forever after.

Initially the Lord Mayor, Sir Thomas Bloodworth, thought it was all a big fuss about nothing – 'Pish,' he said, before returning to his bed, 'a woman might piss it out' – and indeed a mere nine lives were lost in the four days and nights that the flames burned. However, in other regards the impact of baker Thomas Farriner carelessly neglecting to properly douse his oven was without precedent. With pre-Fire London being what a more recent writer has described as 'one endlessly overlapping line of highly flammable dominoes,' 400 acres within the city walls were quickly reduced to little more than scattered heaps of ash and stones (along with another 36 beyond them). Within that area 87 out of 109 churches and 44 ancient livery halls were destroyed, and an incredible 13,200 houses were reduced to smouldering rubble leaving thousands of Londoners camping out under rags with nothing to eat and nothing to eat it off or with.

Faced with such scenes of destruction an estimated 100,000 of them left the capital never to return, nearly a third of the pre-Fire population and roughly equivalent to that proportion of the city which had been obliterated by the flames (or pulled down or blown up to create firebreaks). And when another baker, a French Catholic called Robert Hubert, falsely confessed to having started the fire, those who remained wasted little time in dragging his battered carcass to Tyburn and stringing him up.

The fire may have burned for just four days but putting it right – in the end only 9,000 houses and 51 churches were ever rebuilt – was to take more than half a century. Even then the law-abiding majority of London Catholics had to wait until 1831 – more than a century and a half after the flames had burned themselves out – before the inscription on the base of the Monument (erected 'the better to preserve the memory of this dreadful visitation') was corrected by having the reference to the 'Popish frenzy, which wrought such horrors' finally chiselled out.

Where is London's **most religious** building?

It's hard to ignore the case made for the one at the corner of Brick Lane and Fournier Street, E1. These days no. 59 is known as the Jamme Masjid Mosque, a simple, chaste but elegant Georgian rectangular brick box with tall arched windows. Inside is a prayer hall large enough to accommodate 4,000 worshippers and on its façade a brief but slightly strange Latin inscription on the sundial which reads, *Umbra Sumus* – We Are Shadows. Strange, that is, for a mosque and of course that is the point for this area – currently known as 'Banglatown' but bound eventually to be renamed again – has over the last several centuries seen successive waves of immigrants move in, set up home and then move on. And as the population of this vibrant corner of the East End has changed, so has no. 59 evolved to meet those changes.

The building we see today was originally built in 1743 as La Neuve Eglise, the new church, intended to serve as a place of worship and education for a thriving Protestant community of skilled Huguenot silk-weavers. Since the 1680s they had been arriving here in considerable numbers after fleeing Catholic persecution at home in France, and their legacy can be seen everywhere hereabouts. Not just in several of the street names (Fournier among them) but in the distinctive design of a compact grid of beautifully restored terraced houses, tall and narrow and with many still showing the large top-floor windows which 250 years ago would have enabled the weavers to work for as long as the dying evening light allowed.

Though initially a self-contained community, within a couple of generations the Huguenots were largely assimilated and more widely dispersed across the capital. (The crest of Wandsworth Borough Council, for example, still contains

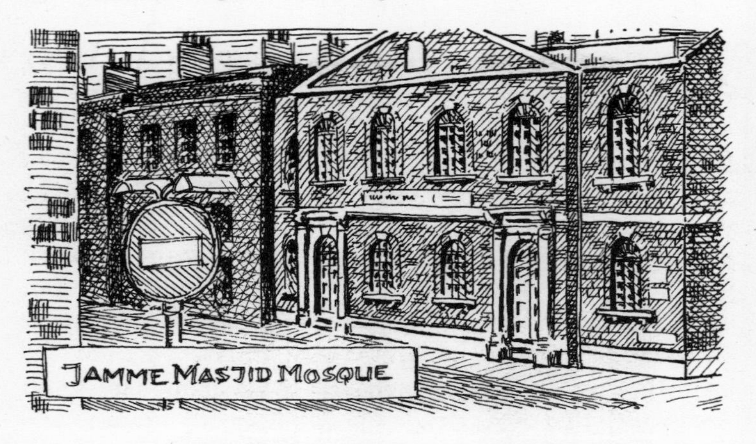

a row of blue dots or *gouttes azure* representing the tears and suffering of local Huguenot settlers.) In 1809, no longer requiring their own church or schools, they sold the building to the London Society for Promoting Christianity Among the Jews. This new organisation had four aims for what now became the Jews' Chapel, namely: to declare from it the Messiahship of Jesus to Jews; to teach the Christian Church about its Jewish roots; to encourage the physical restoration of the Jewish people to the Land of Israel and to encourage the Hebrew Christian-Messianic Jewish movement. When this failed, as it was always sure to do, the building was once more sold becoming, in 1819, a Methodist Chapel.

The Methodists had strong links in the area – John Wesley lived nearby, on City Road – but by 1897, with the local Jewish community growing fast as Yiddish speakers fled Tsarist pogroms, the building changed hands yet again. Now renamed the Machzike Adass or Spitalfields Great Synagogue, it remained in Jewish hands until the 1960s when its congregation in turn began to leak away from the area, many of them to the more prosperous suburbs of north-west London – the so-called 'bagel belt' of Hampstead, Golders Green and Hendon – after which the Great Synagogue closed its doors.

In 1976, however, it reopened once again and today, especially on a Friday, literally thousands of shoes spill out onto the street as the residents of Banglatown crowd into what for now at least is one of the capital's largest, liveliest and best attended mosques. How long it will remain so is anyone's guess, for even if the local Bangladeshis don't assimilate they too are sure one day to disperse into the suburbs.

Why is **Kensington** bigger than **Kensington & Chelsea**?

Property snobbery, pure and simple. Despite the fact that it's the most densely populated local authority in the entire country – with a staggering 13,244 residents per square kilometre making it more than 54 times more congested than the national average – people still keep crowding into the much vaunted Royal Borough of K&C. Stranger still, if they find they can't quite make it – say, if they're stuck out in neighbouring Hammersmith & Fulham, or worse still Brent – they'll probably just lie and tell everyone they live in Kensington anyway.

Estate agents were initially to blame, of course, but thereafter it's down to that class of punter who takes more pleasure from boasting about his or her home than living in it, and who somehow sees more prestige in a postcode than in the merits or otherwise of the flat or house itself.

Not of course that this habit is restricted to the streets and squares around W8. Far from it: failing to see the humour, the quiet anguish, the rather sad desperation, in a telling description of a flat (in Jack Rosenthal's magnificent 1985 monument to property snobbery, *The Chain*) as 'virtually Belgravia, more or less . . . Belgravia Borders, anyway . . . *abutting* Belgravia Borders,' teeming hordes of brick-and-mortar wannabes across the capital have become well practised at talking up their tiny corner.

Kilburnians insist their flat's really 'Brondesbury borders' or Queen's Park, bits of Holloway leak into Islington, and the outer reaches of Peckham elbow their way into leafy Dulwich.

But this kind of thing happens nowhere more than when it comes to Kensington. Kensington proper we all know: it's Kensington Gardens, Kensington High Street and of course the academic and scientific quarter which clusters around the Royal Albert Hall and the celebrated museums at the heart of good old South Ken'.

But Olympia? It's not even in the right borough! Neither of course is so-called West Kensington. Originally everyone knew it as North End – as in the north end of Fulham, the district being well inside in Hammersmith & Fulham – and until the turn of the last century it was still being described officially as 'a modern district within the parish of Fulham.' It stayed that way too, right up until a slump in property sales prompted a pair of – oh, fancy that – estate agent-developers to begin lobbying the Metropolitan District Railway in the hope of changing the name of the station from Fulham North End to 'West Kensington'.

Eventually they got their way, but then went bust a couple of years later anyway. Today though, even people living a good 10–15-minute walk away from that station – i.e. right next door to Shepherds Bush Tube – are still insisting that, somehow, they live in Kensington. Chances are that a few of the really sad ones actually walk the wrong way too, travelling through the rain to the wrong station every morning just to reassure themselves that, yes, they really do live in Kensington even though they know that everyone else knows that actually they live somewhere altogether different.

Where is **London's** only **Nazi** building?

It's a long way short of their most significant failing, but in the 1930s Germany's National Socialists really had no great understanding or appreciation of architecture. Also, few if any genuinely inspired architects, particularly once they had gained control of Dessau, home of the now celebrated Bauhaus school of industrial design. Declaring the iconic establishment as a whole to be 'Jewish' and 'Oriental', and branding its trademark stripped, clean, modern and confident design ethos 'decadent', the Nazis forced its staff and students to leave and then closed the school for good in 1933, the year Hitler was voted in to power.

The Führer's fantasies about creating a 1,000-year Reich nevertheless required him to build something concrete, not least to signify the spiritual and cultural rebirth of his race of so-called *übermenschen*. As an admirer of Imperial Rome – keenly indulging himself in the spurious belief that the Italians were an 'Aryan' race – he managed to ignore the fact that the Germanic tribes were historically very much the enemies of Rome. Instead he sought to emulate their powerful architectural style with his own, rather severe and empty version of the neo-Classical.

Mostly though he was keen to build bigger buildings than anyone else had – in the usual, unthinking way of most new regimes and all dictators – and in the loathsome, self-regarding Albert Speer he found just the man to assist him. One of their first commissions together, for example – the new Zeppelinfield stadium and parade ground in Nuremberg which was immortalised in Leni Riefenstahl's propagandist *Triumph of the Will* – could accommodate 340,000 people. Quickly promoted to *Generalbauinspektor*, Speer's German Stadium was to have been bigger still – seating 400,000 – with another rally ground in the pipeline for half a million. His Volkshalle assembly hall was to be similarly vast, the dome expected to be 1,000ft high – modelled on Rome's Pantheon but sixteen times larger – while Berlin's new triumphal arch, Speer assured Hitler, would be so big that the Arc de Triomphe would fit comfortably inside its opening.

Happily, however, most of Speer's maniac designs were never built, and today it's pleasant to reflect that very little of his work even survives besides a double row of lamp-posts in

Berlin's Straße des 17. Juni and part of the Nuremberg stadium mentioned above. (Oh, and a Soviet war memorial which the Russians built using stone ransacked from Speer's bomb-wrecked Chancellery.)

Regrettably he died a free man and of natural causes – in London, as it happens – although it seems unlikely that on that final trip, in 1981, he found time to visit 8–9 Carlton House Terrace. As the official residence of the Prussian Legates from 1849, and of their successors, the German Ambassadors until the start of the Second World War, this is the only building in London to have been designed or altered by a Nazi.

At the outbreak of hostilities the ambassador was one Joachim von Ribbentrop who was keen for Speer to design something characteristic of the Third Reich's brand of brutalist architecture to be plonked right at the heart of the British Empire. In this he was unsuccessful – Speer didn't even visit London until 1973, when he attempted to enter the country under a false name – so Ribbentrop had to settle for having the interior remodelled by his wife around a heavy marble staircase which was donated by fellow fascist Benito Mussolini.

Happily she was prevented from making any alterations to the handsome exterior, but inside the job was thorough enough with various swastikas and other pieces of Nazi iconography being worked into the fabric and decoration of the Nash-designed Terrace. Apparently they're still there too, although the Royal Society, which has occupied the building since 1967, is sadly not about to allow anyone to start lifting the carpets and having a good old poke around to find out for sure.

Who owns more **paintings** than the **National Gallery**?

We all do, strange as that might sound. Today the National Gallery has around 2,300 works of art, ranging from the thirteenth century to the nineteenth, all of which are housed in

a building by the comparatively little known architect William Wilkins. You know the one: with its small dome and slightly fussy turrets, its design was described by the architectural historian Sir John Summerson as looking 'like the clock and vases on a mantelpiece, only less useful.' William IV similarly thought it 'a nasty little pokey hole,' while Thackeray – being slightly more engaged with the arts – likened it to 'a little gin shop of a building.'

It's big enough to get lost in, however, and there's certainly plenty to see on its walls. It's probably fair to say too that most of us think it's the biggest collection in the country, being the *National* Gallery and all. But in fact London has one substantially larger – even though most of us never get to see it. That last factor makes it tempting to term it the National 'Ungallery', but the collection in question – totalling more than 13,500 works, thus making it nearly six times the size of its more famous sister – is more correctly called the Government Art Collection.

Like the National Gallery it belongs to you and me, not the government. And like the National Gallery it includes a great number of historically important works – paintings, sculptures and other valuable artefacts. But unlike the National Gallery most of the paintings and sculptures in the collection remain all but unknown to the average gallery-goer, most obviously because the average gallery-goer doesn't even know the collection exists.

Among those lucky few who do, art lovers and tax payers alike, it's fair to say that the GAC continues to arouse not a little ill-feeling. That's mostly because a lot of the works hang in the offices of politicians, diplomats and Whitehall officials rather than anywhere the rest of us can get to see them. It doesn't help either that the GAC's own website still declines to disclose its actual location – which is a bit rich when you think the whole thing costs the public something over half a million quid a year, yet appears to offer little benefit beyond providing for the private pleasures of public servants walking the corridors of power.

Admittedly, since 2008, things have loosened up a bit, and nowadays the premises of the GAC (in a cul-de-sac off Tottenham Court Road, but don't tell anyone) is even very occasionally prepared to welcome in the ordinary Joe. That's the good news. The bad news is they only do it three times a month, you have to be a member of an 'established group (maximum 20)' to qualify, not just an interested tax-paying individual, plus you have to book ahead for one of the rare evening slots.

At least it's free – I mean other than the half a million you already stump up every year – and because that same website doesn't make it particularly easy to find the relevant telephone number, we'll do it here instead: 020 7580 9120.

What and where was **Bedlam**?

Variously known throughout its long history as St Mary Bethlehem, Bethlem Royal Hospital of London, Bethlehem or simply Bethlem, its best-known nickname 'Bedlam' – known even to those who do not realise that it still exists – fails to do justice to what is almost certainly the world's first and oldest institution specialising in the containment and latterly treatment of the mentally ill.

Today it's in Beckenham in south-east London, but when it was first founded by Simon FitzMary in 1247 – as a priory for the sisters and brethren of the Order of the Star of Bethlehem – it stood in Bishopsgate Street on a site now occupied by part of Liverpool Street station. By 1330 it was a hospital, admitting its first 'distracted' inmates from 1357, but even by the standards of the time the conditions were dreadful with the first 31 inmates being manacled to the wall or floor and whipped or ducked underwater whenever the noise became 'so hideous, so great that they are more able to drive a man that hath his wits rather out of them.'

In the early days the few considered neither violent nor a danger to themselves were, according to some histories, allowed out during the day and even licensed to beg. In 1557, with England's religious orders now dissolved, it became a royal hospital. Controlled by the city authorities and governed by Bridewell, a combined prison, hospital and workhouse, what this meant in practice was that day-to-day management was in the hands not of medical men but of a keeper, who received payment for each inmate from the relevant parish, livery company or – on occasion – family members.

The resulting neglect was so obvious that in 1620 even the inmates rebelled and complained to the House of Lords with the result that in 1675 the hospital was re-established in a fine set of new buildings (by the genius Robert Hooke) at Moorfields. Not until 1700 did the inmates become patients, however, and it was another twenty-five years before a distinction was drawn between those who might be curable and those who clearly were not. But even then a penny would buy access to the cells – proper wards were still some way off – the public being promised a show (often sexual in nature and not infrequently violent) and advised to bring their own sticks for poking inmates through the bars. As a further inducement to such deplorable behaviour, Tuesdays were free, and the number of visitors nudged 100,000 before it was finally agreed that the practice tended to 'disturb the tranquility of the patients' and ought really to stop.

In 1815 Bedlam moved again, this time to St George's Fields, Southwark, into a splendid new building by Sydney Smirke, author of the original Carlton Club in Pall Mall and younger brother of the architect of London's finest piece of Greek Revival architecture, the British Museum.

Here the so-called unfortunates were allowed a library and (with the most criminal and dangerous patients being removed to Broadmoor) regular dances were soon being held at which the sexes were allowed to mingle. Then, in 1930, the hospital moved into its fourth new home – at Beckenham, where in 1997 Bedlam celebrated a truly remarkable 750th anniversary – with the old one being assigned to the new Imperial War Museum.

2

THE RIVER

How **old** is Old Father **Thames**?

A mere 58 million years young. The name refers to the spirit of London's great river, of course, although the waters actually rise hundreds of miles away in the Cotswolds and for their first 57 million years or so came nowhere near London.

Back then the Thames followed an altogether different path, through Hertfordshire and much of East Anglia before flowing by modern-day Ipswich to join the much larger Rhine (of which it was technically a tributary) and the Meuse and Scheldt. Indeed it was only relatively recently that the formation of a massive ice sheet – during the Quaternary Ice Age, approximately 450,000 years ago – dammed the river forcing it to reroute further south.

At that time the river is thought to have had its source even further west in Wales, but even now its extent is terrific, the river system as a whole collecting some 5.2 billion litres per day from more than 3,750 miles of tributaries covering a catchment area of 5,924 square miles. Flowing for around 215 miles before exiting into the North Sea – and meandering to such a degree that at various different times it heads north, south, east and west – it is by far England's longest river, if only because a portion of the slightly longer Severn lies over the border with Wales.

The word Thames is thought to be the second-oldest geographical name in the language – linguistically only Kent has a longer history – and perhaps because of this its origins are quite obscure. To Julius Caesar in 54 BC it was already the Tamesis, probably meaning the dark river, and in Middle English it became the Temese. It has moreover always been pronounced with a simple 't', one suggestion being that the 'th' spelling was added later, during the Renaissance, perhaps to reflect a connection with the Greek river Thyamis from which region the Celts were for a long time (quite mistakenly) thought to have come. To further add to the confusion, in Oxford only it is known as the Isis, this stretch merging with the River Thames south of Dorchester to become the Thame-Isis or Thames.

Just as the Romans prayed to Father Tiber, so the early Britons prayed to the Thames as a defensive barrier, a means of transport and for centuries to come a valuable source of food and work. In this connection a statue of Old Father Thames can still be seen at St John's Lock, Lechlade – by Rafaelle Monti, it was created for the Great Exhibition of 1851 – and along the length of the river a body of evidence has been found for the existence of shrines and sacred sites and groves. Indeed even in our own century new evidence of the river's sacred role continues to come to light with Christians occasionally baptising each other in its waters, and the discovery (as recently as 2004) of a Hindu shrine near Chelsea Bridge. Three years earlier London also witnessed the recovery of a headless male torso near Tower Bridge, its ritual dismemberment thought to have had gruesome voodoo connections.

How **big** does a **boat** have to be for **Tower Bridge** to be raised?

For nearly 1,500 years London Bridge, or some version of it, was the most easterly crossing point on the Thames but in 1876, with congestion on the river worsening by the month and the population of East London climbing at an alarming rate, the authorities realised that they could no longer ignore the problem. By this time there were plenty of other bridges across the Thames, but they were all upstream. The Corporation of the City of London recognised that it faced a huge challenge in determining how to build a bridge downstream of London Bridge without disrupting the all-important river traffic in what was at this time the capital of a truly global empire.

To solicit and evaluate new ideas, an official Special Bridge or Subway Committee was formed, its various members agreeing that the design for the new crossing should be thrown open to public competition. More than fifty design ideas were duly submitted, but they were nearly all unsuitable with even the great Sir Joseph Bazalgette failing to fully grasp the need for adequate headroom if shipping was to be unaffected.

In fact it wasn't until late 1884 that a winning entry was finally received, John Wolfe-Barry and the city's own architect Horace Jones producing what was agreed to be a workable solution. While aesthetically pleasing – its neo-Gothic style was thought unlikely to offend the Tower of London – it was also highly practical in that it would clear the water by more than 130 feet. Jones and Wolfe-Barry's design was for an opening or bascule bridge, with a vast central span to allow boats to pass unhindered as the road traffic moved up above. Despite its deliberately antiquated appearance, it was also technically hugely advanced, taking a full eight years to complete with five major contractors called in to assist and a total of 432 construction workers putting their shoulder to the task.

To support the vast, towering structure, two massive piers were sunk into the river bed and more than 11,000 tons of steel assembled into a sturdy framework for the twin towers and the walkways strung between. To produce a more finished appearance (and to protect the steel from the inevitable problems of corrosion) the whole structure was then clad in a pleasing mix of Cornish granite and Portland stone.

The word bascule being derived from the French for see-saw, the bridge depended on a series of great counterweights and a complex system of hydraulics to raise and lower the road sections. Until 1976 it was actually steam-powered – a third steam engine was installed during the war in case enemy action succeeded in disabling one – but it now relies on oil and electrical power to lift the two sections from road-horizontal to fully-raised (at 86°) in just one minute.

With shipping no longer coming right into London, most vessels travelling upriver these days have no difficulty passing beneath it so that where once the bridge was raised up to 50 times a day it now opens no more than 1,000 times annually. Often this is to accommodate visiting cruise ships or naval vessels, but more often it is for much smaller yachts with a mast or superstructure of 29ft or more. Any such boat wishing to enter or leave the Upper Pool can ask for what's called a 'bridge lift' by writing to the Bridgemaster, faxing or telephoning at least 24 hours in advance of their arrival. Hordes of spectators are guaranteed on such occasions, and on both banks of the river, and even now there is no charge for the service.

How many **islands** are there in the **Thames**?

Excluding the Isle of Dogs and of Grain, because they're not really islands, rather more than you'd think, with the 97 listed here shown in the order you would encounter them if you took the time to row upstream from the North Sea. They range from the relatively large, flat, 36 square mile expanse of Sheppey in Kent to any number of long, skinny aits or eyots, the majority of which have simply built up over hundreds of years through a gradual accumulation of silt. Most are uninhabited, a good few aren't even very interesting except as small nature sanctuaries, but the list serves to underline what a major watercourse is the River Thames – and to remind Londoners that, like life itself, it doesn't just begin and end within the M25.

Isle of Sheppey
Two Tree Island
Canvey Island
Lower Horse Island
Frog Island, Rainham
Chiswick Eyot, Chiswick
Oliver's Island, Kew
Brentford Ait, Brentford
Lot's Ait, Brentford
Isleworth Ait, Isleworth
Corporation Island, Richmond
Glover's Island, Twickenham
Eel Pie Island, Twickenham
Swan Island, Twickenham
Trowlock Island, Teddington
Steven's Eyot, Kingston upon Thames
Raven's Ait, Kingston upon Thames
Boyle Farm Island, Thames Ditton
Thames Ditton Island, Thames Ditton
Ash Island, East Molesey
Tagg's Island, Hampton Court
Garrick's Ait, Hampton
Benn's Island, Hampton
Platt's Eyot, Hampton
Grand Junction Isle, Sunbury
Sunbury Court Island, Sunbury
Rivermead Island, Sunbury
Sunbury Lock Ait, Walton on Thames
Wheatley's Ait, Lower Sunbury
Desborough Island, Shepperton
D'Oyly Carte Island, Weybridge
Lock Island, Shepperton
Hamhaugh Island, Shepperton

Pharaoh's Island, Shepperton
Penton Hook Island, Laleham
Church Island, Staines
Hollyhock Island, Staines
Holm Island, Staines
The Island, Hythe End
Magna Carta Island, Runnymede
Pats Croft Eyot, Runnymede
Friary Island, Wraysbury
Friday Island, Old Windsor
Ham Island, Old Windsor
Lion Island, Old Windsor
Sumptermead Ait, Datchet
Romney Island, Windsor
Black Potts Ait, Windsor
Cutlers Ait, Windsor
Firework Ait, Windsor
Deadwater Ait, Windsor
Baths Island, Eton Wick
Bush Ait, Windsor
Queen's Eyot, Dorney
Monkey Island, Bray
Pigeonhill Eyot, Bray
Headpile Eyot, Bray
Guards Club Island, Maidenhead
Bridge Eyot, Maidenhead
Grass Eyot, Maidenhead
Ray Mill Island, Maidenhead
Boulter's Island, Maidenhead
Glen Island, Maidenhead
Bavin's Gulls, Maidenhead*
Formosa Island, Cookham
Gibraltar Islands, Marlow
Temple Mill Island, Hurley
Frog Mill Ait, Hurley
Black Boy Island, Hurley
Magpie Island, Medmenham
Temple Island, Henley-on-Thames
Rod Eyot, Henley-on-Thames
Ferry Eyot, Wargrave
Poplar Eyot, Wargrave
Handbuck Eyot, Wargrave
Phillimore Island, Shiplake
The Lynch, Lower Shiplake
Hallsmead Ait, Lower Shiplake
Buck Ait, Sonning
Sonning Eye, Sonning
View Island, Reading
De Bohun Island, Reading
Fry's or De Montfort Island, Reading
Pipers Island, Reading
St Mary's Island, Reading
Appletree Eyot, Tilehurst
Poplar Island, Tilehurst
Nag's Head Island, Abingdon
Andersey Island, Abingdon
Lock Wood Island, Nuneham Courtenay
Fiddler's Elbow, Sandford-on-Thames
Rose Isle, Kennington
Osney Island, Oxford
Fiddler's Island, Oxford

* Bavin's Gulls comprises four separate islands.

Has anyone ever **swum** the **Thames**?

As a foolish teenager the author once jumped off Kew Bridge – crikey, that hurt – and there must be plenty of folk who've swum from one side to the other. (These days there is even an imaginative adventure-holiday outfit called www.swimtrek.com which organises two-day tours for anyone with a pair of trunks and a desire to explore the safer, non-tidal stretches.) But when it comes to swimming the entire length of the Thames – meaning all 200-plus miles – the only one so far is Lewis Gordon Pugh.

One Sunday in August 2006, Pugh – variously a lawyer, SAS officer, polar explorer, environmental campaigner and keen endurance swimmer – stepped ashore to become the first person ever to swim the length of the Thames from its source to Southend. The feat had taken him three weeks, his principal aim being to highlight a World Wildlife Fund climate change campaign, although in the process he also broke the previous record set in 2005 by charity fund-raiser Andy Nation who swam 147 miles from Lechlade to Teddington to raise money for the excellent Anthony Nolan Bone Marrow Trust.

Braving ferocious swans during his watery, cross-country epic, as well as submerged shopping trolleys, wayward boats,

searing summer temperatures, sunburnt shoulders and even Tony Blair, the 36-year-old Pugh – who unusually has also swum in both the Arctic and Antarctic Oceans – was forced to run the first several miles from Kemble to Lechlade as these days the Thames in summer is often barely a trickle up to this point. But thereafter he took to the water, swimming the equivalent of half a Channel crossing every single day, before washing up on the Essex coast.

How **clean** is the **Thames**?

Few of us have either the stamina of a Pugh or the determination, and indeed until relatively recently swimming around in the Thames – at least anywhere downstream of Staines – would have been hazardous in the extreme.

For centuries the London reaches of the Thames comprised nothing less than the world largest open sewer. With London the planet's largest city until it was overtaken by New York in the 1930s, the unpleasant reality was that everything which flowed into the network of pipes running beneath the streets eventually emptied into the Thames, mostly via less substantial rivers such as the Effra, Westbourne and Fleet. In this regard things had been bad enough in the Middle Ages, but as the population of the city grew from less than half a million in 1801 to nearly 2.5 million less than 50 years later, the system of waste disposal (such as it was) simply couldn't cope.

The situation worsened still further as a growing middle-class raced to equip their homes with the last word in advanced domestic appliances – namely Thomas Crapper's patented water-closet ('a certain flush with every pull') – so that by June 1858 *Hansard* was reporting that conditions in the House of Commons Library and Committee Rooms were now such that members 'were utterly unable to remain there in consequence of the stench which arose from the river.'

Already by then it had been the case for decades that as many people who fell in the soup were poisoned as drowned; and while gentlemen making the Grand Tour frequently complained that clothes 'washed in Rome smelt ever after of the Tiber' one would have had to have been quite demented even to consider laundering so much as a rag in the toxic green-brown scum which was the River Thames.

The repository not just of crumbling sewers but also of tons of dung every day, guano, rotting fish carcasses from Billingsgate and the varied discards of the tanning, tar and slaughter-house industries, by 1848, when as many as 400 Londoners a day were dying of cholera, the Thames wasn't even fit for fish. The river's salmon, for example – long considered a bellwether of water purity – had disappeared from the Thames back in the 1830s. With many more species following suit as the decades wore on, it was to take nearly a century and a half before London awoke to the reality of this and made a genuine attempt to bring life back to its major river.

The efforts continue even now, more than £6 million having been spent since 1979 reintroducing salmon to the Thames in the hope that eventually they will not simply head downstream and off to Greenland but return here to breed. To note that the scheme was always intended not so much as to please anglers as to demonstrate to Londoners and visitors alike what was once a running sewer is now more or less clean, but those early attempts failed miserably.

A few fish were hoiked out on the end of a line, and in August 1983 Russell Doig made the front page with a six-pounder. But many more died, or simply disappeared, and none actually appears to have spawned so that when Bloomsbury-based vegetarian Roger Baker wrote to *The Times* asking how a picture of Doig brandishing a dead fish demonstrated that the river was a safe place for its brothers and sisters to live, he seemed to have a point.

That said, it's not all bad news, for the Thames really is cleaner now and while we'll probably never see a return to medieval times – when tens of thousands of salmon ran the river every year, together with trout, shad, lampreys, eels, flounder and even the odd sturgeon – well over 100 different species have been recorded at least once between Fulham and Tilbury in recent years. These are listed below.

Anchovy
Angler Fish
Barbel
Bass
Black Sea Bream
Bleak
Blue Mouth
Bream
Brill
Bullhead
Butterfish
Carp
Channel Catfish
Chub
Coalfish
Cod
Conger Eel
Crucian Carp
Dab
Dace
Dory
Dragonet
Eckstrom Topknot
Eel
Flounder
Garfish
Goby (8 types)
Goldfish
Goldsinny
Grayling
Gudgeon
Gurnard (4 types)
Haddock
Hake
Herring
Lampern
Lamprey
Lesser Weever
Ling
Loach
Lumpsucker
Mackerel
Minnow
Mullet (4 types)
Norway Bullhead
Perch
Pike
Pilchard
Pipefish (6 types)
Plaice
Pogge
Pollack
Poor-Cod
Pouting
Ray, Sting
Roach
Roach-Bream Cross
Rockling (5 types)
Roker
Rudd

- Ruffe
- Salmon
- Sand Eel (3 types)
- Sand-Smelt
- Scad
- Scaldfish
- Sea Horse (2 types)
- Sea Scorpion (2 types)
- Sea Skipper
- Sea Stickleback
- Shad (2 types)
- Smelt
- Smooth Hound
- Sole (2 types)
- Solenette
- Sprat
- Stickleback (2 types)
- Tadpole-Fish
- Tench
- Tompot Blenny
- Trigger-Fish
- Trout (2 types)
- Web Catfish
- Whiting (2 types)
- Wrasse (2 types)
- Zander

What was the **worst** ever **disaster** on the river?

Ask around and nine out of ten will give you the sinking of the *Marchioness,* the occasion when a party boat of that name sank with 130 revellers on board after being struck by the Thames dredger *Bowbelle* in August 1989. In all 51 drowned, including the skipper, but – horribly memorable though this was – it is dwarfed by the dreadful events which unfolded on the same river on 3 September 1878.

That evening the SS *Prince Alice*, a paddle steamer named after a daughter of Queen Victoria, was making one of its celebrated 'Moonlight Trips' from Swan Pier near London Bridge to Gravesend and back. With tickets priced by the London Steamboat Company at just two shillings a head, many hundreds of Londoners were crowded on board to enjoy the facilities of Rosherville Gardens in the Thameside Kent town. Spirits were high when, returning to London, the *Alice* encountered a much larger vessel, a screw-steam coal-hauler called the *Bywell Castle* which was on its way to collect a load from Newcastle.

In sight of North Woolwich Pier, at about 7.45 p.m., confusion arose as the two boats prepared to pass each other on the water. With an experienced pilot on board, Captain Harrison, skipper of the *Bywell Castle*, prepared to follow the traditional Thames route rather than passing oncoming vessels on the port side. Unfortunately, this confused the captain of the *Alice* who made for the north bank. Master William Grinsted thereby took his vessel across the bows of Harrison's ship and in doing so forced him to change course once again to pass astern. This sudden change caused Grinsted to switch again, inadvertently bringing the *Alice* onto a hard collision course with the much larger *Bywell Castle*. Immediately Harrison threw his engines into reverse and at full speed, but it was too late: contact was made, the *Princess Alice* split literally in two and within four minutes the steamer had gone down into the water with her passengers trapped in the sinking hull or thrown into the river.

At the time of course the average Londoner could not swim. As previously noted, neither was the river as clean as it is today, particularly on this stretch where raw sewage was routinely dumped into the Thames from nearby Beckton. Nevertheless, as many as 170 people were somehow pulled alive from the water by Harrison and his crew, but unsurprisingly the vast majority perished. Literally hundreds of corpses were eventually pulled from the wreckage when the two halves of the stricken vessel were salvaged; but many more were never recovered despite a generous bounty of 5*s* being offered to Thames watermen for each body they successfully recovered from the river.

In all as many as 640 people are thought to have drowned that evening, including the captain of the *Princess Alice*. Subsequently, when it proved impossible to identify all of them, 120 of the dead were buried in a mass grave at Woolwich Old Cemetery, a memorial cross being erected to mark the spot. It is still there today, 'paid for by national sixpenny subscription, to which more than 23,000 persons contributed'.

Sadly, within just two months Princess Alice, Grand Duchess of Hesse, was herself dead (at 35, of diphtheria) and the number of pleasure trips on the Thames also declined markedly as a consequence of the accident, eventually forcing the London Steamboat Company into bankruptcy. Captain Harrison never took to the water again, and less than five years after what remains Britain's worst ever civilian nautical tragedy, the *Bywell Castle* too sank with all hands – in the Bay of Biscay, while hauling coal to Africa.

What was the **Prospect** of **Whitby**?

Regardless of the time of year you get an interesting view from any of London's historic riverside pubs, Wapping's famous Prospect of Whitby included, although from Wapping there is no prospect whatever of seeing Whitby. In fact the name is a reference to a Tyneside collier which in the nineteenth century was in the habit of tying up nearby. Prior to this the pub had been called the Pelican, also the Devil's Tavern on account of its unsavoury clientele of smugglers and thieves who had been drinking here since the 1520s. Pepys is said to have been a regular (the Ancient Society of Pepys still meets at the bar), Whistler and Turner immortalised the view of the river from the rear, and Judge Jefferies drank here when he wasn't presiding over the famous 'Bloody Assizes' which followed the abortive Pitchfork (or Monmouth) Rebellion of 1685.

Sir Hugh Willoughby is also believed to have set sail from the steps to the rear of the tavern in 1533 in a bid to discover the North-East Passage to China: his frozen corpse and those of his crew were discovered about a year later by Russian fisherman. More recently Del-Boy Trotter dropped in looking for Uncle Albert when the old sea-dog went missing during an episode of *Only Fools and Horses*, but as to why the pub was named after a quite unremarkable vessel is still something of a mystery.

What was the **last wooden bridge** over the Thames?

Battersea Bridge, which was built by Henry Holland and remained in place until as late as 1887. Holland's client was John, 1st Earl Spencer, Lady Di's forebear having earlier commissioned him to remodel Althorp when the roof of his ancestral home fell in. In London Lord Spencer had envisaged building a splendid bridge of iron and stone, but unfortunately funds were tight, outside investors being reluctant to risk more than £1,500, and having only recently acquired the rights to the sixteenth-century foot ferry the cheapskate earl decided to settle for a cheaper, simpler bridge made almost entirely of wood.

When the structure first opened for business in 1771 as a toll bridge it was for pedestrians only. The following year, to boost profits, wheeled traffic was permitted to cross whereupon it became apparent just how makeshift the whole thing was. Whistler and Turner reportedly found it romantic – there's a statue of the former at the northern end, and presumably it looked the part in paintings – but Holland's design was far from good, the materials clearly inadequate to the task, and the discovery during its construction of a quantity of Roman-era corpses at one end probably didn't auger too well either.

It was also highly unpopular from the start with both the bridge-travelling public and the boats which passed underneath. When a number of collisions required two piers beneath it to be removed, several iron girders had to be fixed to it to restore its rigidity. The murder of Sarah MacFarlane as she was crossing the bridge in 1844 was another big disincentive for would-be users, especially when it emerged that the tollkeeper had watched the murder take place but decided not to intervene as the murderer, Augustus Dalmas, had paid good money to use the bridge. Nor did the press like it either, *Punch* finding it 'an expression of the barbarism of Gothic ages' while a guidebook to the nineteenth-century capital dismissed it as 'a deformed, dangerous and hideous looking structure'.

The earl and his cohorts nevertheless managed to recover all or most of their investment – those braving the bridge on foot were charged a penny, with carts paying the full shilling – but business dropped off markedly in 1858 following the completion of what is now called Chelsea Bridge. With the authorities fearful that with falling tolls routine maintenance might no longer be carried out, the bridge was compulsorily purchased by the Board of Works and following a bit of public sector prevarication finally knocked down and replaced by the green and gilt cast- and wrought-iron structure we see today.

This too gets hit by boats from time to time, most recently in 2005, and in 1979 somebody was murdered while crossing it. However, mostly Londoners seem to like it, although motorists will know that as the narrowest road bridge in the capital it can still be something of a bottleneck.

Who was **Doggett**, of the celebrated **coat** and **badge**?

The University Boat Race may be more famous, but more venerable – and by a nautical mile – is Doggett's Coat & Badge. A foundation date of 1715 – the light and dark blues didn't get going properly until 1839 – means it's not just the world's oldest continuously contested boat race but also the oldest sporting competition of any sort held anywhere in the United Kingdom.

The race was established by an Irish actor-manager and 'staunch Revolution Whig' by the name of Thomas Doggett, who wished to somehow celebrate the first anniversary of King George's arrival on the throne and was inspired by the example of a courageous young oarsman who rowed him home on a stormy night.

His choice was a sculling race on the Thames, held on or near 1 August each year, with the competitors to be drawn exclusively from the ranks of watermen 'just out of their apprenticeship'. The course was measured from London Bridge to Chelsea, the prize being a coat in the orange-red livery of the Whigs together with a large silver badge representing 'Liberty' and depicting the running horse of Hanover.

Keen that his race 'be continued annually on the same day for ever', Doggett bequeathed a not inconsiderable sum of money to the Worshipful Company of Fishmongers enabling the Livery to administer the event ever since from its splendid riverside hall.

Doggett's insistence on the race being run 'for ever' has been taken sufficiently seriously that even two world wars have not been allowed to halt it: the 1915–19 competitions were delayed but then held in 1920 and the 1940–6 races were rowed back-to-back in 1947. Tidal conditions have called for some variation, however, meaning the date of the race has on occasion had to vary, and today's craft are also somewhat lighter than the unwieldy passenger-carrying wherries and clinker gigs which Doggett would have known.

Otherwise the test is every bit as severe as ever it was, with competitors required to negotiate 4 miles and 5 furlongs of water – at 7,400m that's a good deal longer than the university boys have to do – and to pass beneath no fewer than eleven bridges. Of course they also row solo instead of in an eight, and once you've seen them hard at it you quickly appreciate why the winners are traditionally welcomed into the élite of rough-water oarsman as members of the 22-strong team of Royal Watermen who guard the crown at the State Opening of Parliament. Also why they are still revered long after the original impetus for the race, a chance for Mr Doggett to cock a snook at the loathed Jacobite pretenders, has been all but forgotten.

Who are the **Mudlarks**?

In late 2009 the *Daily Telegraph* reported the case of Steve Brooker, a keen amateur metal-detectorist, who had found a seventeenth-century leg iron weighing 17lbs on the south bank of the river at Rotherhithe. In the opinion of an archaeologist from the Museum of London Docklands the artefact in question was too costly to have been thrown away, and with the ring still locked shut the likelihood was that the leg iron had probably been attached to a would-be escapee who had drowned in the mud and filth of the Thames foreshore.

Perfectly preserved, and almost entirely free of rust as the high-quality iron would have been protected from corrosion by thick, air-excluding black mud, the find was one to bring joy to the heart of any mudlark, the given name of the modern-day amateur treasure hunters who search the exposed bed of the Thames when the tide goes out.

Of all those to have stuck with the 1970s metal-detecting fad, erstwhile Rolling Stone Bill Wyman is probably the most famous, striding out from his medieval manor house in Suffolk in search of gold and other goodies and making some outstanding finds in recent years. Indeed, from the muddy banks of the tidal Thames to the Highlands and Islands, the classic image of the hobbyist is someone like Wyman – a lone operator with his tweeting detector in one hand and a trowel in the other – although since 1980 a number of like-minded enthusiasts have come together to form the Society of London Mudlarks.

Named after the original band of ragged Thameside foragers – barefoot scavengers who like generations of totters, gong farmers and rag-pickers managed to eke out a precarious living on the fringes of Victorian London society – today's Mudlarks are in effect the capital's official treasure-hunters in that they are licensed by the Port of London Authority to use their equipment on the Thames and to dig the mud between the tides. Working together in this way has its advantages in an area where the tide can frequently be treacherous, and the mud sticky enough to bog down the unwary or ill-informed. But the licence carries significant responsibilities as well as rights, requiring the Society's members to take any finds to the Museum of London to be recorded rather than indulging in the so-called 'shovel-and-run' activities of yore.

Of course in the case of major finds there has long been legislation in place to guard against the worst excesses of the freebooters, most recently the wonderfully named Treasure Act (1996) for gold or silver items believed to have been hidden by an owner who intended to return at a later date to recover them. The task of determining whether something is treasure trove or was simply lost or mislaid is left to the coroner at an inquest – and his judgement is crucial since anything designated as such automatically becomes the property of the Crown.

Finders are at least rewarded for their efforts, with something approximating to the market value of their finds and the knowledge that the artefact in question will end up in the British Museum or a similar institution. One of the Museum of London's best Mudlark pieces, indeed, is a solid silver fifteenth-century collar made of interlocking S-shaped links of the sort given by the Lancaster Plantagenets to their ambassadors and other high Court officials. 500 years on, one can only guess at how it came to be consigned to the slime, although one suggestion is that it may have been hastily discarded during the Wars of the Roses when allegiance to one side or the other could have had fatal consequences.

Sadly, perhaps, a typical Mudlark find is neither gold nor silver but rather more domestic in tone with the best discoveries being made between London and Blackfriars Bridges, on the edge of the medieval City, where for centuries Londoners would have thrown their rubbish. Not that all of it would be classified as rubbish today, for as the museum's John Clark is at pains to point out many less obviously valuable items of the sort which crop up all the time – lower-value coins, buckles, pilgrim tokens – can still tell an interesting tale.

'Sometimes,' he says, 'one gets clusters of finds which suggest a story. For instance, when a whole group of sixteenth-century gentleman's weapons was found, suggesting there was a recognised place where you got rid of daggers.' Similarly a hoard of counterfeit coins from about 1500 was found in another spot, the offence of being caught in possession of these being so serious at the time that the holder perhaps caught fright and tossed them into the river before he or she could be arrested and executed.

Which part of **Kent** lies **north** of the **river**?

Though now situated in the London Borough of Newham, and almost entirely encircled by East Ham, the riverside enclave known as North Woolwich was administratively part and parcel with Woolwich – which of course lies on the opposite bank of the river – and as such, for more than 800 years, was technically a part of the county of Kent.

Though separated by the water the two are still linked, by the Woolwich Foot Tunnel and the wonderful if slightly anachronistic Woolwich Free Ferry. They are thought first to have been brought together after the Norman Conquest when one of the Conqueror's lords, one Hamon de Crevecoeur, was granted land on both sides of the Thames at this spot in 1086. Almost certainly this was done to enable him to enjoy the benefits of taxing cross-river traffic, the politically astute Hamon being at the time both Sheriff of Kent and a 'dapifer' or royal steward.

In 1899, however, major administrative and boundary changes meant that North Woolwich was brought into the new County of London, somewhat unusually given its distance from the centre of the capital since the county at that time comprised just the twelve inner London boroughs. In fact it wasn't until 1965 that this anomalous position was finally corrected, with the district being transferred to the London Borough of Newham as part of the creation of the much larger administrative entity we now know as Greater London.

How many **bodies** do they pull out of the **Thames** each **year**?

Around fifty a year, of which approximately forty are almost certainly suicides most of whom will have jumped off one of the bridges. Most suicides occur during the winter months, with a peak around Christmas; in summer months cheerful drunks are more likely to jump in while larking about or even to wander in to cool off without considering the possible consequences.

Either way the unenviable task of recovering them falls to the Marine Support Unit – what used to be called the Thames Division – which has a special mortuary facility at Wapping police station where the bodies are held for identification.

In the eighteenth and nineteenth centuries this was the spot where murderers and pirates were hanged, their bodies being left to be washed over by three tides before they were removed. Today the equally grim mortuary can be seen from passing pleasure boats, a tall square frame covered with blue tarpaulin which conceals a large stainless steel bath used to store the deceased. After being recovered, these are numbered DB1, DB2, etc – short for Dead Body, with the numbering being reset to one on 1 January each year.

The numbers brought here have remained pretty constant in recent years, but nevertheless represent quite an improvement over time, if only because the levels of river traffic are now much lower than in previous centuries. In March 1932, for example, the Home Secretary was reported in the Parliamentary record *Hansard* to have been made aware of 158 bodies being pulled from the river in a single year from the reaches covered by the

City of London and Metropolitan Police. Concerning these, the coroner recorded death by drowning or an open verdict for 56, with 46 suicides and a further 39 dying through what was termed 'misadventure'. The remaining 17 were presumably murder victims.

According to some estimates if you fall in during the winter months you could have as little as two minutes to live, the shock of the cold water being enough to paralyse your limbs so that you quickly sink and drown. Thereafter bodies deteriorate surprisingly quickly, often not just through decay but as one policeman puts it because 'the water is very cruel, the river is tidal [and] you get hit by boats and barges and attacked by seabirds.'

The sharp bend in the river as it rounds the Rotherhithe peninsula brings many bodies ashore close to Limehouse, but where they wash up can depend on many factors, including the victim's size, their clothing and even what they have eaten. The temperature and flow of the water also has an impact, with another officer observing that in summer the bodies tend to surface more quickly 'because the gases are released faster'. Even so, it is not uncommon for a body to have been in the water for two to three weeks before it is finally found.

3

ROYALTY & CEREMONIAL

Who gets a **21-Gun** Salute?

The short answer is the monarch, guns having been fired to honour the sovereign since primitive artillery first made an appearance in London in the mid-fourteenth century. It didn't always go according to plan – in 1460 a curious and incautious James II of Scotland stood too close for safety 'and was unhappely slane with ane gun' – but the tradition has endured, albeit in recent years without the use of live ammunition.

Today the guns sound over London on the following days: the queen's accession day; Her Majesty's birthday and official birthday; coronations and successive Coronation Days; the Duke of Edinburgh's birthday; and to mark the State Opening of Parliament. Royal births are also marked in this manner, along with those occasions when visiting Heads of State are presented to the sovereign.

The traditional 21-gun salute involves half-a-dozen Great War pattern 13-pounders being pulled at full gallop to Hyde Park and fired by the men of the King's Troop, Royal Horse Artillery. Afterwards an additional 20 rounds are fired because Hyde Park is Crown property, with an even more resounding 62 rounds being discharged if the firing takes place at the Tower of London. Here the total comprises the basic 21 plus 20 because it too is Crown property – besides being a fortress the Tower is a royal palace – with a further

21 rounds being fired as a compliment to the monarch 'from the City of London'.

At the Tower they use slightly more modern weapons too, the officers and men of the Honourable Artillery Company – a volunteer or Territorial unit – discharging their 62 rounds from a number of Second World War 25-pound howitzers. As the oldest military body in the country, the HAC also fires an exceptional 101-gun salute when the crown is first placed on the head of a new sovereign, but this is of course a very rare occurrence so that the best known ceremonial firing is the one which takes place on Remembrance Sunday. On that day at 11 a.m a single shot is fired on Horse Guards' Parade to signal the beginning of the 2 minutes' silence with another single precisely 120 seconds later.

Why is **Buckingham Palace** so called?

Foreign ambassadors posted to London are still appointed to the Court of St James's – a reminder of what remains the senior royal residence even though no member of the royal family has lived in Henry VIII's red-brick Tudor warren for two centuries or more. Instead the sovereign's actual London residence is a short walk along the Mall, Buckingham Palace having been fashioned around the core of the Duke of Buckingham's old town house when this was acquired by the Crown – in the person of George III – in 1761.

Then called Buckingham House it had been purchased not for George at all but as a retreat for his queen, Charlotte, who was delivered of fourteen of their fifteen children in what soon became known as the Queen's House. It was only with the accession of Victoria in 1837 that the head of state moved in permanently, the name reverting to Buckingham Palace perhaps because 'Saxe-Coburg-Gotha Palace' might have sounded a mite too foreign to the majority of patriotic Londoners.

Since becoming a royal palace it has been modified in stages over many years – by the likes of John Nash, Edward Blore, Thomas Cubitt, and most recently Sir Aston Webb – as a consequence of which it is no longer recognisable as the ducal home it once was. Some of the interior modifications are surprisingly recent too, for example the conversion in 1938 of a small pavilion at the rear to accommodate an indoor swimming pool.

Much of the earlier work was undertaken to address Victoria and Albert's concerns that it was too small for their rapidly growing band of princes and princesses. With nine children, forty grandchildren and in time several dozen great-grandchildren, they were probably right to be concerned, although the finished result – 828,818sq ft of floorspace accommodating 775 rooms including 240 bedrooms and 78 bathrooms – might have been slightly overdone.

Princess Margaret didn't think so, and always claimed to have found the place quite cosy. But Queen Victoria often complained about the distances involved in moving from one wing to another and, finding the whole process 'so fatiguing', as a widow withdrew almost completely to Windsor Castle and Osborne on the Isle of Wight before public opinion eventually persuaded her back to SW1.

Edward VII evidently wasn't much of a fan either, describing it as a sepulchre and barely more comfortable than Balmoral which he referred to as 'the Highland Barn of a Thousand Draughts'. George VI similarly likened it to 'an ice box' while his big brother Edward VIII was still complaining about its 'dank, musty smell' long after he'd been reduced to a duke and exiled to France. As for the present sovereign, she hasn't really expressed an opinion one way or the other, leaving her Prince Philip to observe on more than one occasion that Buckingham Palace isn't really theirs anyway, but merely 'a tied cottage'.

Between 1838 and 1841 Buckingham Palace was visited on several occasions by an intruder nicknamed 'The Boy Jones' (whose notoriety even gained him a mention in Dickens) and in 1982 a 32-year-old called Michael Fagan scaled a drainpipe and tripped a number of alarms before spending a few minutes sitting at the end of Her Majesty's bed having a chat. More recently, however, the Palace has begun welcoming members of the public on a more official footing with visitors happy to pay £16.50 being admitted at certain times during the summer months to the majestic state rooms.

Who or what is **Black Rod**?

Correctly known as the Gentleman Usher of the Black Rod, the gentleman in question is essentially the usher or doorman to the House of Lords. The equivalent to a Serjeant-at-Arms, his most celebrated task is to summon members of the House of Commons to the upper chamber for the State Opening of Parliament in order to hear the 'Queen's Most Gracious Speech'.

On that day, with the State Crown travelling in a separate carriage and guarded by the Royal Watermen, Her Majesty arrives at Westminster to address both houses. Parliamentary privilege having ruled against any monarch personally setting foot in the Commons since Charles I's unsuccessful attempt to arrest five MPs in 1642, Black Rod – as the Queen's messenger – is traditionally greeted by having the door rudely slammed in his face. He – and so far it has always been a he, the post for the last 100 years having gone to a succession of retired senior military figures – is forced to knock three times before eventually being permitted to issue the invitation.

The name of the office comes from the staff or rod he uses to knock on the door, an ebony rod topped with gold lion. Once the door is finally opened, the Crown's representative can still only request that Members attend on Her Majesty rather than demanding it, although even these days it is hard to imagine many members of the lower chamber choosing not to do so.

What is the **Temple Bar** Ceremony?

Despite a host of unique privileges and prerogatives – ranging from the right to any whales washed up on the beach to the freedom (still) to dismiss the government, disband the Army, sell off the Royal Navy and give away sovereign territory to a foreign power – it can sometimes seem as if the Queen is not entirely free to do what she pleases in the whole of her realm.

The rest of us, for example, can just drive into the City whenever we fancy. But if the monarch wishes to travel that way he or she traditionally halts at the western boundary of the Square Mile – at the point where Fleet Street meets the Strand – and waits there until the Lord Mayor advances to present her with the City's pearl-encrusted Sword of State.

In fact doing it this way is very much a nicety, and by no means suggests (as many think) that the monarch needs the permission of anyone to enter the City. Called the Temple Bar Ceremony, and involving the monarch pausing briefly before entering London's unique, self-governing financial district, the presentation of the sword is an indication of the City's continuing loyalty to the Crown rather than some kind of formal permission required before the Sovereign Head of State can enter the Square Mile.

The name of the ceremony naturally recalls the Temple Bar, an attractive old stone gateway which stood on this spot until 1870 when – its 400-ton bulk considered an unacceptable impediment to increasingly heavy commercial traffic – it was dismantled and shipped out to Hertfordshire. Rebuilt as a garden folly on the estate of brewer Sir Henry Brent Meux and his wife, it eventually returned to London in 2004 when it was rebuilt in Paternoster Square. Its original location is today marked by a much smaller stone monument, sitting in the middle of the roadway and topped by the City's heraldic griffin.

Why do we **Troop** the **Colour**?

Absolutely the best bit of ceremonial in London – at least until they reinstate the magnificent Royal Tournament – Trooping the Colour marks the sovereign's *other* birthday, the official one, and recalls the days when a British regiment still followed its flag or colours into battle. The practice stopped with the Crimean War but it had a long and honourable history. The colours originally provided something to rally round if a regiment's position became desperate, and since the seventeenth century have been an important focus for the essential *esprit de corps* on which any effective fighting force must depend.

Because of this it was crucial that new recruits be able to identify their own colours in the heat of battle, so the practice of regularly trooping the colour – basically showing it off – was a common one. Today, as a piece of ceremonial, it is much less so, the exercise being now restricted to the Household Division with one of the five foot regiments – Grenadiers, Coldstream, Scots, Irish and Welsh – presenting their colours each year.

The ceremony itself always takes place on a Saturday in June, on Horse Guards' Parade. Since the reign of Edward VII (1901–10) the sovereign has always taken the salute in person – Queen Elizabeth II has traditionally worn the uniform of the appropriate regiment – afterwards carrying out an inspection of some 500 troops. In recent times it has been cancelled only once, when a nationwide rail strike dished it for everyone in 1955.

Otherwise, massed bands many hundreds strong, the sight of the Regimental Colour being carried down the ranks, a march-past by the Foot Guards and the Household Cavalry, and the horses and guns of the King's Troop, Royal Horse Artillery make for a spectacular morning. Thereafter, at 1 p.m., members of the royal family reassemble on the balcony of Buckingham Palace for a traditional flypast by the Royal Air Force and at the end of the day there's even a bit of ceremonial for the horses, each of which is presented with a carrot on a silver salver in the inner courtyard of the Palace.

Demand for tickets to the event always exceeds supply, so to be in with a chance applications for the stands need to be made in January or February – in writing to the Brigade Major, Headquarters Household Division, Horse Guards, Whitehall, London, SW1A 2AX – after which your name goes into a ballot to be drawn out (or more probably not) in early March.

What became of **Charles I's** Executioner?

The fates of the fifty-nine signatories and attendants to Charles I's trial and execution were varied but generally speaking as grisly as one would have wanted. With his son restored to the throne, an Act of Indemnity and Oblivion was passed in order to officially pardon the majority of those who had supported Oliver Cromwell and played a role under the Protectorate. It made several exceptions, however, and of the thirty-one regicides still living Charles II saw to it that six were publicly hanged, drawn and quartered, several others merely hanged, and those who had fled into exile hunted down, extradited and brought back home for further punishment. Finally the bodies of three who had died in the meantime – including the despised Cromwell – were exhumed and publicly beheaded.

But what of the man who actually carried out the deed, the dead king's executioner? Unsurprisingly – the country was by no means uniformly Parliamentarian – his identity was not revealed at the time, nor following the return of Charles II was anyone likely to step forward and identify himself.

The register of St Mary Matfelon, in Alder Street, Whitechapel, however, records the passing of one possible candidate, listing on 2 June 1649 the death of Richard Brandon of Rosemary Lane, a ragman said to have 'claimed the headman's axe by inheritance' from his father, Gregory Brandon, the former common hangman of London. Appended to the church register is a telling line – that, 'This R. Brandon is supposed to have cut off the head of Charles I'. Brandon apparently confessed before dying that he was offered £30 to complete the task 'all in half crowns'. It was likewise said that he had taken from the king's person a white silk handkerchief and an orange stuck with cloves, which he later sold for ten shillings in Rosemary Lane (now Royal Mint Street, in the Minories).

Sadly the veracity or otherwise of this intriguing coda may never be known, as the alleged confession came to light only in a pamphlet published after his death, the anonymous author also maintaining that Brandon's sudden death was occasioned by his own remorse at what he had done. Certainly he could have been responsible for the king's death, having earlier executed a number of other notables, including the Duke of Hamilton, the Earls of Holland and of Strafford, and Archbishop Laud. He is also known to have been asked to take his axe to the king, although it is also quite possible that for obvious reasons he declined to do so or that he performed the task only under great duress.

When is it OK to **break** a **sword** over someone's **head**?

As a general rule the only way to witness an investiture is to be there to pick up a gong yourself, or to be a family member or close friend of someone who is. But frankly it might be more fun to see the opposite.

When the late John Lennon didn't want his MBE any more it was rude but technically OK for him to send it back to the Palace in the back of his white Mercedes. But because a knight was, and still is, created by a formal investiture it remains the case that he can only properly be deprived of that same honour by a process of formal degradation.

Of course this doesn't happen often. Most of us would like to think that KBEs and KGs are usually honourable men, and even in the very early days it seems unlikely that the honour would be forfeit except in cases of the most heinous treason or craven cowardice. But to remind them of this possibility, after an installation of knights at Westminster Abbey, the king's cook would be posted outside. Armed with a large chopper he was instructed to whisper to each knightly neophyte, 'Sir, you know what great oath you have taken, which, if you keep it, will be of great honour to you but, if you break it, I shall be compelled by my office to hack your spurs from off your heels.'

In doing so he was referring to the detail of a knight's degradation, something which would have been performed publicly and with as much ceremony as the original investiture. His spurs would be roughly hacked off and smashed to pieces; his armour, shoes, gloves and coat of arms would have been stripped from his person; and finally the knight's sword would be broken over his head by heralds before he was taken away to be hanged and quartered.

The first to go this way is thought to have been Sir Andrew Harclay, Earl of Carlisle, during the reign of Edward II. In 1468 Sir Ralph Grey of Doncaster is likewise on record as having had his 'gold spurs hewn from his heels'. And in 1621 Sir Francis Mitchell escaped with his head but had his sword broken over it and in the very public arena of Westminster Hall was declared to be 'no longer a Knight but a Knave'. More recently, however, while the severest penalties have still been applied – as late as 1916 Sir Roger Casement was thrown into the Tower and beheaded for treason – the ceremonial aspects seem to have been abandoned. Sir Roger was formally and officially stripped of his knighthood, but there was nary a mention of spurs, gold or otherwise, or indeed a broken sword.

Who lays **flowers** for Anne **Boleyn**?

When it came to beheading wife no. 2, Henry VIII was considerate enough to fork out a not inconsiderable £23 for a skilled French swordsman – apparently doing it that way is slightly less grisly than when it is done with an axe – but curiously made no arrangements for a burial.

Instead, with not even a coffin on order, the former queen's corpse lay on the scaffold on Tower Green until a man – probably just a servant or labourer working in the Tower – found an empty arrow chest, placed her decapitated body inside it, and left it and the head to be buried in an unmarked grave in the adjacent Chapel of St Peter ad Vincula. There it stayed, beneath the floor, unknown and unidentified, until the chapel – the name of which means 'St Peter in Chains' – was being renovated during the reign of Queen Victoria. At that point efforts were made to identify several of the many scores of corpses which came to light, with the results being documented in a number of surveys which were circulated at the time.

In one such, an 1877 report by Doyne C. Bell with the less than snappy title of *Notices of the Historic Burials in the Chapel of St. Peter ad Vincula in the Tower of London, with an Account of the Discovery of the Supposed Remains of Queen Anne Boleyn*, a certain Dr Mouat reported that:

> The bones found in the place where Queen Anne is said to have been buried are certainly those of a female in the prime of life, all perfectly consolidated and symmetrical and belong to the same person. The bones of the head indicate a well-formed round skull, with an intellectual forehead, straight orbital ridge, large eyes, oval face, and rather square full chin. The remains of the vertebra and the bones of the lower limbs indicate a well-formed woman of middle height with a short and slender neck. The ribs shew depth and roundness of chest. The hand and feet bones indicate delicate and well-shaped hands and feet, with tapering fingers and a narrow foot.

No sixth finger then, just an 'intellectual forehead' but it was held to be her, since when a London florist has fulfilled a standing order to deliver red roses to the tomb every 19 May, the anniversary of her brutal death. For well over a century the arrangement was a complete mystery to the Tower authorities, and of course a pleasantly romantic one which has charmed visitors for decades. But then a senior official at the Tower became more than usually fascinated by the tradition, and on his retirement managed to track down some Boleyn family descendents living in Kent who eventually admitted that it was indeed they who had maintained the tradition started by their forebears.

What's so **special** about the **Cullinan** and the **Koh-i-noor**?

Even the smallest diamond is remarkable. The name says it all – from the Greek *adamas*, 'invincible' – with the youngest being at least 990 million years old and some of the older ones apparently closer to 3.2 *billion*. But some are more remarkable than others, and by happy chance all the very best are incorporated into Britain's Crown Jewels.

The most famous, the Cullinan, was discovered more than a century ago on a Transvaal farm only recently acquired (by Sir Thomas Cullinan and his partners) from a poor old Boer called Willem Petrus Prinsloo. It was and remains the largest diamond ever found: fully 4in long and weighing 3,106 carats – an incredible 1.3lbs. When first brought to the surface it was assumed to be a rough lump of glass secreted in the mine wall as a practical joke.

When the *Transvaal Leader* suggested that the great lump be presented to Edward VII, Sir Thomas accepted £150,000 for his find – to put that into some kind of perspective, £100 was at this time a perfectly respectable annual salary for a professional man – and on 7 November 1907 in the presence of the doubtless slightly green queens of Norway and Spain it was presented to the king at Sandringham. Thereafter the terrible responsibility for cutting it fell to Joseph Asscher of Amsterdam who studied the huge stone every day for three months before finally raising his cleaver's blade in preparation for doing the deed.

At the first blow the hardened steel blade actually broke, and on the second Asscher is said to have fainted clean away. But fortunately the stone had been split exactly as planned and over the coming months his skilled hand and eye produced the 530.2 carat pear-shaped Cullinan I or 'Star of Africa' for the Royal Sceptre (this is still the world's largest cut diamond) together with three more giants totalling almost the same weight, and 101 much smaller stones weighing up to 18.85 carats apiece.

All 105 gems found their way into the Crown Jewels, and have since appeared at every coronation and important state occasion. At each of these they share the limelight with another fabulous royal jewel, and one which perhaps even better expresses diamond's enduring magic and mystique, namely the Koh-i-Noor.

At a mere 108 carats and set into the State Crown, the name means 'Mountain of Light', and its history is the longest of any known gemstone. More than 700 years ago, in 1304, Sultan Ala-ed-din is said to have captured the jewel from the Raja of Malwa whose family had already held it for many generations. Changing hands several times thereafter – it is thought to have been set in the famous Peacock Throne of Shah Jehan – it eventually left Persia for the Punjab, coming into the possession of the powerful Honourable East India Company whose governing council in 1849 decided to present it to Queen Victoria.

The decision made, the British Commissioner put it in his waistcoat pocket and somehow forgot about it. But reminded of it six weeks later – by what? by whom? – Sir John Lawrence at last remembered to send it to London, the jewel arriving just in time for the Great Exhibition of 1851. It was eventually presented to Queen Victoria by the dispossessed 9-year-old Sikh Maharaja Dalip Singh Sukerchakia – his subordinate role in the ceremony a potent symbol of British rule in the Indian subcontinent – and has since been worn by every British sovereign as once it was worn by moguls, shahs and rajahs.

Have the **Crown Jewels** ever been **stolen** from the **Tower**?

Well Oliver Cromwell pinched most of them and had the collection melted down after the establishment of his Commonwealth in 1649. But like most dictators throughout history he managed to convince himself that he was acting for the public good, within the law rather than as a common criminal. If we accept his view of things then the only person one can really point the finger at – and he didn't quite pull it off either – is the splendidly named if rather mad, bad and dangerous Thomas Blood in 1671.

Variously described as a colonel and a captain – although in all likelihood he was neither – Blood sounds a charmer but was something of a desperado. Born in Ireland, where his army officer father was Member for Ennis, Blood Jnr switched sides more than once during the Civil War and when the music stopped somehow contrived to find himself on the winning side. Accordingly, in 1650, he was rewarded with a grant of land confiscated from the Royalists, married well and looked set for life – at least until the Restoration a few years later when his lands were repossessed.

Thereafter his life more or less fell to pieces, and he embarked on what the historian Christopher Hibbert describes as an 'extralegal career spanning two decades.' In 1663, for example, he became entangled in a plot to seize Dublin Castle and when that went wrong was forced to go on the run, fleeing first to Holland and then to England where he set himself up as a doctor. In 1670, after a few years lying low, he made another foolish move, deciding to kidnap the Duke of Ormond, Lord High Steward of England, whom he intended to hang at Tyburn.

This too failed and a year later he conceived his boldest and most ambitious caper yet, a plan to break into the Tower of London to steal the Crown Jewels which at this time, bizarrely, were kept in a cupboard in the basement of the Martin Tower. Their custodian was one Talbot Edwards, a slightly feeble, 76-year-old former soldier who was in the unfortunate if understandable habit of showing them to visitors in order to supplement his meagre stipend with a few extra shillings.

In April 1671 Edwards received a request to see them from an elderly, bearded Doctor of Divinity and his suspiciously stubble-chinned 'wife'. By a process of flattery and trickery effected over several days, the two succeeded in catching the old boy off-guard, gagging him, tying him up and stabbing him in the belly before making off with the loot.

Fortunately they didn't get very far and, after a scuffle on Tower Wharf, most of the jewels were recovered although one crown was stamped flat thereby knocking a couple of stones from their mounts. Edwards was eventually to receive a £200 bonus for his trouble, although he died of his wounds before he had time to enjoy it, while Blood – insisting, 'it was a gallant attempt, however unsuccessful! It was for a crown!' – continued to refuse to discuss the matter with anyone but his king.

And it is here that the story takes its most extraordinary turn, with Blood apparently managing to so charm the monarch with his version of the tale that when he left the royal presence after their time together, the rogue had not only had his lands restored to him but also managed to collect a substantial lifetime pension of £500 a year.

It's a great story – and who to play the lead? Sid James? Alan Rickman? – although even now many feel that the king's role in it has been inadequately explained. Many suspect that he had put Blood up to it as part of a jolly drunken wager between chums, or that he was planning to split the proceeds with the Irishman in order to help alleviate his own increasingly pressing financial needs. The truth is, after nearly three and a half centuries, the likelihood is we shall never know.

4

BUSINESS

Which is the **oldest firm** in London?

The smart money's on the Whitechapel Bell Foundry, the East End factory which can trace its history back nearly 600 years, has an entry in the *Guinness Book of World Records* as the oldest manufacturing company in the country, and a string of master founders going back in an unbroken line all the way to Robert Chamberlain in 1420.

At that time Henry V was on the throne and it was still to be almost another three-quarters of a century before Columbus set sail for America. But fast forward to today and, having been producing church bells through an astonishing twenty-seven reigns, the foundry is still going strong and seems to have been responsible for just about all the famous bells which have ever been made.

That means not just Big Ben and the eighteen which gaily chime the quarter-hour outside Fortnum's (see p. 83) but also America's Liberty Bell, those hanging in the National Cathedral in Washington DC, and the Great Bell of Montreal. In fact the foundry first went into the export business as long ago as 1747. That was the year a set of bells was despatched to St Petersburg in Russia, with the first American sale being made seven years later when they produced a substantial set for Christ Church, Philadelphia.

The present Grade II-listed buildings date from only 1670, almost certainly replacing premises which fell to the Great Fire and which had previously been a wayside inn known as the Artichoke.

Perhaps the most remarkable thing about the place, however, is not what they manufacture but that they manufacture at all; that one can still find an old-fashioned metal-bashing venture – albeit a highly skilled, highly distinguished one – barely half a mile from the Bank of England.

It's also extraordinary to find a business still doing precisely what it did centuries ago, and relying on the same skills and much of the same sort of equipment. It's still family-run too, and has many of the same customers it had several centuries ago, including the authorities at Westminster Abbey who have been on its books since the 1500s.

In all that time the foundry has strayed from bell-making only once. During the Second World War, bell metal being close in composition to gunmetal, the workforce was required to direct its talents to making machine castings for the Ministry of War and bits of submarines for the Admiralty. Thereafter it was a return to business as usual, with much of the period immediately post-war being spent making up for lost time by replacing the many famous peals lost to enemy action – including the bells of St Mary-le-Bow and St Clement Danes.

What was the **Great Beer Flood** of 1814?

Boys will be boys, size does indeed matter, and once the eighteenth-century City brewer Samuel Whitbread had thrown down the gauntlet by making the centrepiece of his impressive Chiswell Street brewery a magnificent, positively Brobdignagian beer barrel it was inevitable that rival brewers would quickly try to outdo him.

The building in which Whitbread placed his big barrel was sufficiently grand for his Porter Tun Room to still be a major City venue for official dinners and functions. But very soon after its completion in 1760 a competing brewer went one or two better, Henry Thrale building a vat so monstrous that he was able to invite no fewer than 100 bigwigs to dinner actually inside the barrel.

Nor did the competition stop there as before long another brewing Henry, name of Meux, commissioned the largest one yet: some 22ft high, and nearly three times as wide, his was said to be large enough to brew in excess of one million pints of porter at one go. This made it large enough for 200 to sit down to dinner – 'Stick that in your pipe, Mr Thrale' – and by 1814 Meux's vat was ready to be installed alongside another one almost as large at his Horse Shoe Brewery in the West End.

The brewery stood on the junction of Tottenham Court Road and Oxford Street, where the Dominion Theatre is today, and together the pair would have held something like a quarter of a million gallons. Weighing-in at well over a thousand tons, the barrel's wooden staves were held together by a series of enormous iron hoops, one of which – noticed a workman on the fateful day – was slightly cracked. Unfortunately he wasn't that concerned: at 500lbs the iron hoop was after all very large and the crack only small. There were moreover another twenty-eight hoops on the same barrel to support the wood should the faulty twenty-ninth ever give way . . . which, alas, it did on the afternoon of 16 October. It did so with such a loud report that the resulting explosion could be heard 5 miles away and produced a jet of liquid sufficiently powerful to fatally damage the vat next door. As yet more pungent liquid poured forth, the brewery wall gave way sending a tidal wave of beer into the street and literally washing away several neighbouring buildings while sending pedestrians spilling down the street.

In all, nine people died as a consequence of the split barrel, some crushed by falling walls, others literally drowned in beer, and yet others being killed in the inevitable stampede as people headed for the gutters in order to drink their fill before dying of alcohol poisoning. Among the many more who were seriously injured were patients in a nearby hospital who rioted when the injured were brought in (in the mistaken belief that they were being denied free beer clearly being distributed in other wards). Then, later in the day, as hundreds crowded into the house where the dead had been laid out, yet more injuries were sustained when the floor of the house collapsed sending everyone down into the cellar.

Eventually, when the mess had been cleared up and the dead buried, the brewery was brought to court only for the case to be thrown out when the jury found there was no case to answer: the judge declared that the Great Beer Flood was an Act of God. With the directors thus found not culpable for the ensuing death and chaos, Meux's Brewery Co. Ltd successfully appealed to parliament for a refund of the duty it had paid on the beer which was lost – and continued brewing on the same site until 1922, albeit in smaller, stronger barrels.

Which is London's **smartest bank**?

Coutts everyone knows, because obviously 'the Queen banks there'. Barings is equally celebrated, but for completely the wrong reasons. And Child & Co. has nice cheque books although like Coutts it is just a division of RBS. In fact all of

Britain's famous old family banks have gone now, either swallowed up by the big banking groups or gone phut after the odd fatally stupid investment decision or as a consequence of their inability to keep pace with a much faster-moving financial world.

All except C. Hoare & Co., that is, whose wonderfully discreet way of doing business is such that all most of us know of 37 Fleet Street is that the front door can only be locked from inside meaning that – 24 hours a day, and 365 days a year – at least one of the partners has to be on the premises to slide the bolt across.

If that sounds like an extraordinarily antiquated, bowler-hatted, Captain Mainwaring sort of way to run a bank in the twenty-first century it's worth reflecting that this eleventh-generation family bank is clearly getting something right. How else to explain how, with nine of the founder's direct descendents currently running the shop, it is quite literally the sole survivor of a once-thriving banking industry which at one point numbered more than 4,000 going concerns?

The founder was Sir Richard Hoare, a goldsmith who set himself up in business in the mid-seventeenth century and made the switch to banking in 1672. This was far from being an uncommon move: goldsmiths by definition required secure premises, they were often called upon to provide storage for cash and clients' valuables, and by this time nearly sixty of them around Cheapside were keeping what they called 'running cashes' and lending out surplus monies to customers at a rate of interest.

Hoare's customers in the early days were illustrious too, and included Charles II's wife, Catherine of Braganza, the diarist Pepys, 'Beau' Nash, John Dryden and the portaitist Godfrey Kneller. Later came the actor Garrick (see p. 138), the Prime Minister Lord North, two famous Thomases (Chippendale and Gainsborough), Eton College and Lord Byron. As to who they are today, not much is known beyond the total number – a mere 10,000 – and that like a good London club it is jolly hard to get in. So hard, indeed, that unlike many *very* good clubs the fact that your father, grandfather and even great-grandfather has been accepted may still not be enough to smooth your own path in.

Which is London's **oldest hotel**?

For most of London's long history there were no hotels. Those who could afford them, and could bear to, would put up at an inn; those who couldn't would sleep where they fell. Otherwise the very rich kept their own townhouses for those occasions when they ventured up from the country, while anyone of the middling sort – such as Jane Austen, who stayed with her brother Henry in Sloane Street – would cheerfully sponge off a friend or family member who lived nearer town than they.

Indeed in Austen's day there was reportedly only one hotel in the whole of London which could be called respectable. Converted in 1774 from an old Inigo Jones mansion at 43 King Street, Covent Garden, it became Evans Hotel and Supper Rooms but is now long gone although the building itself survives and appears to be in good order. (In the 1960s the basement was home to the counter-culture Middle Earth club, famous for hosting the likes of Soft Machine and Pink Floyd, The Crazy World of Arthur Brown, The Bonzo Dog Doo-Dah Band, Fairport Convention and Jefferson Airplane.)

Today the oldest surviving hotel in the capital is Claridge's, originally a pair of houses in Brook Street, Mayfair, which opened for business in 1812 under the management of a French chef called Jacques Mivart. He ran it for years before selling out to William Claridge in 1838, Claridge operating for several years under the banner of 'Mivart's at Claridge's' (and then 'Claridge's, late Mivart's') before eventually having the courage to shorten the name and doing very well for himself.

In 1860 the Empress Eugenie put up here during an extended visit, and after she had entertained Queen Victoria on the premises the hotel's reputation was clearly made. Victoria then praised it to her uncle Leopold, King of the Belgians, and for years afterwards it enjoyed a reputation as a sort of unofficial annexe to the Palace. Acquired in 1895 by Richard D'Oyly Carte, theatrical impresario and owner of the somewhat *parvenu* Savoy Hotel, it became a sort of home-from-home for European royalty, and in the words of the Baedeker guide was very much 'the first hotel in London'.

Following the First World War Claridge's provided a useful substitute for those noblemen who could no longer afford to staff and maintain a London home, and during the Second World War it was home to a number of high-profile exiles including the kings of Yugoslavia, Greece and Norway, Queen Wilhelmina of the Netherlands, the Grand Duchess Charlotte of Luxembourg and the President of Poland. Even this fine tally was eclipsed during the Coronation in 1953 when it was rumoured – hotel staff naturally remained tight-lipped about the precise particulars – that no fewer than fourteen crowned heads moved in on a semi-permanent basis. Apparently when someone rang and asked to speak to His Majesty, the girl on the switchboard could only enquire, 'Which one?'

How did **Carnaby Street** become the **centre** of the **World**?

Savile Row is smarter, Bond Street longer, more glamorous and more expensive, Jermyn Street infinitely more varied and interesting – and indeed, until London's first 'boutique' opened there in 1957, Carnaby Street was just another old but boring and rather run-down West End thoroughfare. Running between Regent Street and Soho, its sole claim to fame prior to this had been that Inderwick & Co. once had the shop at no. 45, this being the company which first introduced the Meerschaum pipe to the English smoker.

But two centuries on everything changed forever, Mr John Stephen opening the somewhat naff-sounding His Clothes after an earlier shop in Beak Street had burned down. A Glaswegian and the first person to import Levi's to Britain (at 5 guineas a pop) Stephen chose Carnaby Street because it was close enough to Regent Street but with much cheaper rents. Others soon followed and Stephens was joined by a number of would-be rivals, including I Was Lord Kitchener's Valet, Cecil Gee, Lord John and Mr. Fish – all of them keen to cater for the growing numbers of young people who were adopting the new Mod and Hippie styles.

As a young person's hangout, Soho, with its well-established milk bars and beat culture, was already on the map, and Stephen's clothes were soon being worn by the Beatles as well as by members of the Kinks, Small Faces and Rolling Stones. He had shrewdly noted that theirs was the first generation which didn't wish to dress like their parents, and while he was himself always quite a sober dresser, he soon had loud music blaring out of his doorways with punters being offered pink velvet jackets, hipsters and bright, floral shirts. At a time when Englishmen were finally beginning to take an interest in fashion, and to spend money on their appearance, Stephen's strength was that he was constantly coming up with new ideas. Soon he had no fewer than fifteen shops in this one street alone as well as branches elsewhere in the capital, a report in the *Daily Telegraph* describing, 'mini-kilts for men, elephant-cord low-slung trousers and androgynous flared velvet double-breasted jackets hung alongside kaftans and Aertex shirts on the rails outside his boutiques.'

A relentlessly flamboyant figure – on trips to the US he would routinely be accompanied by his Rolls-Royce, although his white Alsatian dog had to be left behind – Stephen and the street he had colonised soon became synonymous with Swinging London. Liberace played in one of his shops, Petula Clark filmed part of her TV show in another, and having launched a John Stephen Award for Britain's best-dressed guy, the man himself was never short of a big-name film- or popstar pal to present the trophy.

But the real turning point came on 15 April 1966, and the publication in America's *Time* magazine of a cover feature examining the burgeoning Sixties culture and London's leading role in its genesis. Declaring that 'perhaps nothing illustrates the new swinging London better than narrow, three-block-long Carnaby Street, which is crammed with a cluster of the "gear" boutiques where the girls and boys buy each others' clothing,' it set the seal on Carnaby Street's success. Now everyone knew about it – one hip young designer, Ossie Clarke, was claiming to be 'as famous as egg foo yung' – and from across the world they all came to see Carnaby Street for themselves.

Where is London's **oldest shop**?

You could be forgiven for choosing hatter Edward Bates in Jermyn Street, the interior of which has barely altered since it opened for business in 1900. Until its closure in 2010 it looked absolutely wonderful: row upon row of decorative hatboxes; fading yellow newspaper cuttings of the Great and the Good sporting their new Bates hats, caps and panamas; and – surveying it all – the benign gaze of Binks the cat looking down at you from his perch.

The aforenamed feline reportedly wandered into the shop as a stray nearly eighty years ago and, 'admired and loved by everyone', he never left. Stuffed and mounted when he died around the time of the National Strike, he sported the topper and cigar without which, visitors were always told, he was never seen.

But for all its eccentricity the shop itself is actually a relative newcomer. Elsewhere in Jermyn Street J. Floris has shop fittings originally built for the Great Exhibition in 1851, while Bates' next-door neighbour Geo. F. Trumper, replete with dark panelling and lined with gleaming glass-fronted cabinets, looked for all the world like a senior club library rather than a mere barbers shop. Not that there was ever anything 'mere' about George Trumper: appointed Court Hairdresser to HM Queen Victoria, Empress of India, his family has been similarly honoured through five subsequent reigns.

But George's business is, even so, barely a start-up alongside that of James Lock & Co. at no. 6 St James's Street. Very much the oldest shop in London – the adjacent wine merchant, Berry Bros & Rudd is the only one to run it close – Lock inherited a hatter's business from his father-in-law way back in 1676 and moved it here shortly afterwards.

Like Berry Bros it's still family run, and still run the old way too so that when Westminster Abbey needed a new hat for its wax effigy of Nelson they not only ordered it from here (because that's where the old one came from) but were able to check the vain old sailor's measurements in the meticulous records the shop has kept since the turn of the century. The eighteenth century, that is, Nelson having called in immediately before departing for Trafalgar. He came to pay the bill for one of his special Lock hats with a bespoke built-in eye-shade, just as the Duke of Wellington was to wear one of the company's plumed hats ten years later on the field at Waterloo.

It was Lock & Co. too which sold the world's first ever bowler hat, the staff even now insisting that the distinctive protective headgear is called not a bowler but a 'Coke' (pronounced cook) after the Norfolk landowner who ordered several to guard his gamekeepers from overhanging boughs. Apparently when the Hon. Edward Coke, brother of the 2nd Earl of Leicester, arrived in London in 1849 to check his order he placed one on the floor and stamped hard on it twice to test its strength. The rigid felt crown passed muster with flying colours, and he paid 12 shillings apiece for the rest.

Who were **Fortnum** and **Mason**?

There are so many reasons to love Fortnum & Mason: the frock coats; the mingling aromas of the magnificent food hall; the emporium's bespoke roof-mounted beehives; the mere thought of one of those £25,000 hampers bursting with what Dickens described as 'a blossom of lobster salad'; the fact that it's not Harrods; and of course all those royal warrants going back nearly 150 years.

But to many visitors – strolling down Piccadilly to gawp rather than to spend – the best is outside. I mean the famous four-ton clock, of course, which every 15 minutes plays a selection of airs on eighteen bells. Then, once an hour, Messrs Fortnum and Mason make a brief appearance in 4-foot effigies, bowing to each other before disappearing once more into its works.

In 1705 Mr Hugh Mason had a smaller shop behind this surprisingly big one, in St James's Market which had been established to serve the ducal mansions of Henry Jermyn's elegant new St James's Square. However, business really took off when he met Mr Fortnum a year or so later, renting him a room while the latter was employed as a footman to Queen Anne. It seems Her Majesty liked to have fresh candles every night, William Fortnum recognising at once that a quantity of half-used candles – especially half-used royal candles – was a resource not to be wasted.

By 1707, having amassed a tidy sum selling them to the local gentry, he'd handed in his cards at the Palace and gone into business with his friend retailing 'hart's horn, gableworm seed, saffron and dirty white candy'. With fashionable London by this time very much centred on St James's, the two were perfectly placed to influence and profit from the changing tastes of their wealthy, aristocratic neighbours.

As a business Fortnum & Mason quickly prospered, proving itself to be a smart innovator, introducing a postal service for customers in 1794, almost half a century before the General Post Office was even founded, and with collections six times a day. The firm also introduced an early form of profit-sharing in 1846, when a descendent of one of the founders left his fortune to his loyal staff, as well as becoming the first shop in Europe to sell baked beans after buying the entire stock of them in 1886 from an enterprising young man called H.J. Heinz.

Fortnum's is also credited with the invention of the Scotch Egg, which to the irritation of Caledonian sorts everywhere turns out to be no more Scottish than several other innovations to which they traditionally lay claim (such as tartan kilts, bagpipes, and indeed the haggis). The store was also far-sighted enough to provision the early Everest expeditions (with quail in *foie gras*) and those searching for Tutankhamun, as well as sending supplies to officers fighting the Peninsular War and in the Crimea.

Not that things have always gone quite as planned: in the 1920s a much larger branch of F&M was opened in Manhattan – just in time to close again as the Great Depression began to bite. Another on the Isle of Wight fared rather better though, albeit for just one very particular week each August when Fortnum's own motorboat could be seen ferrying supplies from Cowes to Royal Yacht Squadron members on their saltwater palaces floating in the Solent.

Some individual departments in the main store have been fairly short-lived too, including one opened to coincide with George V's 1935 Jubilee. With so many princes and potentates crossing the Empire to be with the king-emperor, the staff at Piccadilly created a special department to accommodate their exotic dietary requirements. Similarly during the Second World War a special 'Officers' Department' was established to provide a respite from bully beef. Such essentials as patent anti-insect powder, silver-plated 'sporks' for eating trench suppers single-handed and even special nickel-silver bayonet tips were soon flying off the shelves.

Where does the **Tube** get its **electricity** from?

By far the biggest single user of electricity in London – using 3.5 per cent of the total, according to Transport for London – the Tube for many decades generated its own electricity at three private power stations in Chelsea, Greenwich and Neasden.

The largest of these, on the river at Lots Road, Chelsea, was coal-, later oil- and then gas-fuelled. In 1905, long before the London Underground became a unified network, it powered the District and Circle lines owned by the hitherto steam-powered Metropolitan District Electric Traction Company. Almost certainly the first steel-framed industrial building in England, and with its four chimneys for many years the tallest in Europe, it remained in service until 2002 giving it the longest continual service life of any power station in the country.

Consuming upwards of 500 tons of coal a day – and cooled by an incredible 60 million gallons of water from the Thames – Lots Road began to work in conjunction with the Metropolitan Railway's plant at Neasden as the network grew to cover more of London. Greenwich came on-line somewhat later, having been commissioned by London County Council to power the city's extensive tram network.

Eventually, however, in-house generation no longer looked quite so smart, with power from the national grid costing appreciably less per unit and Chelsea's attractive riverside location being greedily eyed by developers as land and property prices began to rise. Today, as a result, the network runs on the same electricity as the rest of us, albeit at around 1,225,000,000 Kw/h annually – or enough to keep a single 100w bulb burning for 1.4 million years. With very nearly 15 per cent of this coming from renewable sources by 2008 – not bad given a UK target of only 10 per cent by 2010 – Transport for London insists it is doing its bit for the environment and so, in a sense, are London's hard-pressed commuters.

Why isn't **SW2** anywhere near **SW1** or **SW3**?

With pretty much every business relying on the post to some degree, and with an incredible 100 million letters being addressed to London by the 1850s, it soon became obvious to the Victorians that a new system was needed to subdivide the capital if its postmen were to enjoy even a sporting chance of delivering everything to the correct addresses.

Such subdivisions were soon drawn up and brought into use on New Year's Day 1858, dividing London into ten segments – labelled EC, WC, N, NE, E, SE, S, SW, W, and NW – each of which had its own central head office. Initially it worked well enough, but as London and the demands of commerce grew, so did the amount of mail and the complexities of delivering it.

Within less than a decade the novelist Anthony Trollope, wearing his other hat as a civil servant, was suggesting abolishing both the NE and S postcodes and merging them with their neighbours. (Eventually NE was assigned to Newcastle upon Tyne, with S being used to denote Sheffield.) Further efficiencies came during the First World War, the subdivisions being further subdivided into yet smaller districts with each of these identified by a number as well as the existing letter.

To bring order to the new system the initial subdivisions remained in place, with EC1, WC1 and so on now redesignated as 'head districts'. Thereafter the succeeding numerical values were apportioned alphabetically so that in the SW region, for example, with SW1 as the most central portion being the head district, SW2 was assigned to Brixton, SW3 to Chelsea, SW4 to Clapham, SW5 to Earls Court, SW6 to Fulham and so on.

Put like that it looks, and is, fairly logical; it's only when driving from, say, the Elephant and Castle to Clapham Junction that things seem to go awry when a mere 4 miles or so of reasonably straight main road takes one from SE1 through SE11, SW9, SW8 and then SW4 to finish in SW11. Just as oddly, Havering, Hillingdon, Barking and Dagenham and Sutton are not included as London postal districts at all – even though all clearly fall within the Greater London area – but Sewardstone in Epping Forest does. That's despite it being nearly 12 miles from Charing Cross, and as such way beyond the capital's normal outer boundary. (It's actually 'London E4', should you ever need to know.)

What does **Greenwich Mean Time** Mean?

Mean solar time was legally adopted in Britain in 1792, but the need to properly standardise time across the whole country became more pressing as faster rail travel began to supplant horse and waterborne traffic. Without some standard measure, a westbound train could effectively arrive at its destination earlier than an eastbound one, even if the two were travelling over an identical distance at precisely the same speed.

To avoid this anomaly the railway companies began to set station clocks in accordance with Greenwich Mean Time, this being measured from the brass strip marking the 0° meridian at the Royal Observatory in South London. They did so despite strong objections from the Astronomer Royal, who for a while continued to insist that doing it this way was to perpetrate a lie in those areas where the sun was not directly overhead at noon. (The authorities at Christ Church Oxford were similarly picky, and apparently even now maintain a fiction that one is not late for an appointment until one is five minutes late – a calculation based on the college's longitude of 1° 15' W.)

Other countries eventually arrived at a variety of similar accommodations, but the growth of international trade (and the invention of the telegraph) meant that by the late nineteenth century a genuinely global standard was badly needed. In October 1884 the International Meridian Conference met at Washington DC to devise one, and after some debate managed to agree on a proposal suggesting that the prime meridian be that 'passing through the centre of the transit instrument at the Observatory in Greenwich'.

Somewhat surprisingly the proposal came from the Americans rather than the Brits; somewhat less surprisingly the French objected to it fairly robustly and for many years afterwards continued to print wholly misleading maps showing the 0° meridian passing through Paris not London. In an attempt to mollify them, the conference eventually agreed to a French demand that consideration be given to a new decimal measure of time – an echo of the 1789 revolutionaries' failed attempt to introduce a new calendar in which the day was divided into 10 hours of 100 minutes, each of which was 100 seconds long.

Paris also continued until as recently as 1911 to define what it called legal time as 'Paris Mean Time minus 9 minutes and

21 seconds', but most nations took what now looks like a rather more mature approach and today people around the world know what GMT stands for, even if to many of them the word 'Greenwich' is more or less meaningless and couldn't with any certainty be identified on a map.

5

PEOPLE

Who is the **oldest** known **Londoner**?

The oldest skeletal remains ever found in the Greater London area belong to a man aged 25 to 35 and female aged 30 to 40 which have been carbon-dated to the period 3640–3100 BC. But as these were unearthed at Shepperton – formerly in Middlesex but since 1965 located in Surrey – they are perhaps too far out to be properly considered Londoners.

Instead the most likely contender would have to be the 5ft 2in skeleton of a young woman found in Southwark, a relative youngster at something under 2,000 years old. Laid to rest near Harper Street at some point in the first century AD, she is buried in a simple wooden coffin, nailed shut, with a bronze mirror at her feet and a plain pottery flagon. Her identity, alas, remains a mystery

Who was **London's** first **celebrity chef**?

Creative, innovative, and restlessly energetic, Alexis Benoît Soyer (1810–58) arrived in Victorian London from Meaux-en-Brie by way of Paris, taking the city by storm and becoming by far the most famous cook in the Empire.

Expelled from school, he first found work in a Parisian restaurant and by the age of 20 was employed by Prince de

Polignac at the French Foreign Office until the 1830 revolution persuaded him to quit France and try his hand in England. Recruited to the London household of Prince Adolphus, Duke of Cambridge – tenth child and seventh son of George III, and a younger brother to George IV and William IV – he later worked for the Duke of Sutherland and the Marquesses of Ailsa and Waterford.

In 1837, however, he abandoned private service and accepted the post of *chef de cuisine* at the new and architecturally ambitious Reform Club on the south side of Pall Mall. Earning an eye-popping £1,000 a year, his early arrival at the club meant he was able to assist the architect Sir Charles Barry in the design of the technologically highly advanced kitchens, later marking the completion of their joint venture by preparing a celebratory breakfast for 2,000.

Among the innovations he pioneered at the club were cooking with gas – the street and the club house were among the first in the capital to be lit this way – refrigerators which were cooled by cold, piped water, and ovens in which the heat could actually be regulated. As one visitor 'so favoured as to enter this sanctuarium' breathlessly observed, in Soyer's vast, white domain, dishes were warmed, spits turned and water drawn by 'all-powerful steam'.

However, the Frenchman's ambitions extended a good deal further than feeding a gaggle of middle-class clubmen. Appalled by Ireland's Great Famine of 1847 he went on to design a mobile soup kitchen, travelling to Dublin to serve many thousands of poor while penning a volume called *Soyer's Charitable Cookery* and giving away the proceeds. Two years later, another invention which he called the Magic Stove enabled people to cook food wherever they were, even travelling on a train, while another of his books – *A Shilling Cookery for the People* – was directed at a public which could afford neither elaborate kitchen equipment nor exotic ingredients.

Like many latter-day celebrity cooks he contrived at least once to lose a substantial fortune after overreaching himself, resigning from the Reform Club and opening his modestly-titled 'Gastronomic Symposium and Monster Pavilion of All Nations' on a site opposite the Great Exhibition in Hyde Park. The experience cost him £7,000, or around half a million in the devalued currency of our own times. But Soyer soon recovered and was back in business, travelling to the Crimea entirely at his own expense to address the problems of military catering. Designing the Soyer Stove for cooking in the field, a device which remained in service until late into the twentieth century, he also worked with Florence Nightingale to completely reorganise the provisioning of Army hospitals, and at the time of his early death – with seven books under his belt – was busy designing a completely new type of mobile cooking carriage for the British Army.

Who was the last **Prime Minister** to fight a **duel**?

In the long and not always entirely honourable history of duelling, no fewer than four English Prime Ministers have sought satisfaction in the traditional manner, at least two of them doing so long after the practice was outlawed. The first was William Petty-FitzMaurice, 1st Marquess of Lansdowne – commonly known to history as the Earl of Shelburne, the title he held while Prime Minister in 1782–3 – who fought a Colonel Fullarton in 1780. His successor William Pitt the Younger had a go at it too, in 1798. Then in 1809 George Canning found himself squaring up to the Secretary of State for War and the Colonies after he and Lord Castlereagh became embroiled in an argument over where the troops should best be deployed. Canning favoured Portugal, Castlereagh the Netherlands, and despite the former never having fired a pistol, the two met at dawn where the novice was rewarded with a ball in the leg from the better man.

Perhaps the most extraordinary, however – not least as his name has come down to us as a byword for common sense and probity – was the Duke of Wellington. When the 9th Earl of Winchilsea accused His Grace of having 'treacherously plotted the destruction of the Protestant constitution', the duke responded immediately by challenging him to a duel. On 21 March 1829 the two met on Battersea fields accompanied by their seconds, Sir Henry Hardinge (for the duke) and the Earl of Falmouth for Winchilsea.

According to contemporary reports Wellington took aim but fired wide while Winchilsea kept his arm down and refused to return the fire. Accounts differ as to whether he and Falmouth had stage-managed the whole thing beforehand although Wellington, not noted for his aim, afterwards claimed that he had missed deliberately. Winchilsea denied this version of events but, with honour apparently satisfied, he sent the duke a written apology and the matter more or less ended there.

Despite the illegality of the act – their guns were hidden under a hedge, and the duellists took care not to be seen by some nearby labourers – the incident eventually played well for Wellington. Finding his reputation enhanced by this display of courage and 'manly forebearance', his Duchess was able to tell their son, the Marquess of Douro, that 'the Mob were . . . abusing your father, now they are cheering him again.'

Who had the **worst** ever **mockney** accent?

Edward VIII, as Prince of Wales, liked to affect a dreadful fake cockney accent to annoy his fastidious father – which it certainly did – but by common consent the award belongs to Dick Van Dyke in *Mary Poppins* if only because the prince generally did it in private whereas Van Dyke broadcast it to the world. Dishonourable mentions also go to Cary Grant (in *None But the Lonely Heart*) and Richard Attenborough for *The Guinea Pig*. As relatively local lads – born in Bristol and Cambridge respectively – both could reasonably have been expected to have put on a better show.

Why isn't **James Greathead** more famous?

At the foot of Cornhill, hard by the Royal Exchange, there stands a towering memorial to James Greathead (1844–96), an entire traffic island in itself and taller than a double-decker bus. Even so many people simply don't notice it, and of those who do it's a fair bet that most have got no idea who James Henry Greathead was or what, if anything, he did for them.

It's true that he warrants an official English Heritage blue plaque, on the front of 3 St Mary's Grove, Barnes, where he lived between 1885 and 1889. True too that when workers on the Waterloo & City Line discovered a surviving portion of his genius invention – the Barlow-Greathead Shield – it was restored in his memory and left *in situ*. But the fact remains that only a fraction of the more than one billion excursions undertaken on the Tube each year are made by people who have heard of him, and that fewer still comprehend that without him millions of Londoners would likely still be struggling to work by tram.

Greathead was an engineer, probably Great Britain's most under-appreciated species of professional, and after being educated in South Africa and at Westbourne Grove was first employed on P.W. Barlow's pioneering Tower Subway at the age of just 24. Designed to run little cable cars under the Thames before being converted to a foot tunnel and attracting a million users a year, the Subway succeeded where Brunel failed largely thanks to the aforementioned tunnelling shield. It's still in use today too, running communications cables beneath the river more than 140 years on, with its curious cylindrical brick entrance standing close to the ticket office for the Tower of London.

Essentially a mobile, wrought-iron tube with a similar diameter to the tunnel under construction, Greathead's shield enabled a route to be excavated through soil too soft or too fluid to support itself before the new tunnel is lined with a conventional support structure of concrete, brick, cast iron or steel. During construction the shield slowly inches forward as the working face is excavated, enabling a permanent tunnel lining of cast iron segments to be fitted into place with no obvious danger to the workforce from a sudden or partial collapse.

The idea was not Greathead's alone, something similar having been patented by Sir Marc Isambard Brunel and Lord Thomas Cochrane in 1818 after Brunel observed the activities of the common shipworm *Teredo navalis*, a wood-boring mollusc. But working with Barlow it was Greathead who got it to work properly, cleverly refining and improving Brunel's basic concept; principally by making it circular in cross-section – meaning it was simpler and stronger – whereas Brunel had, somewhat curiously, fixed on a clumsier rectangular form.

Along the way Greathead himself patented many more significant improvements too, including the use of compressed air and forward propulsion using hydraulic jacks, as he moved on to much larger tunnelling projects such as the new City and South London Railway which now forms part of the Northern Line.

As the world's first electric tube railway, and so very much the prototype not just for the modern London Underground but for numerous metro systems in Europe, the Americas and beyond, James Henry Greathead thus created something which as well as changing the face of London is still in use a century and a half later. But is he celebrated? Barely at all.

Who was London's **first** Lord **Mayor**?

Everyone knows the story of Dick Whittington, some even appreciating that, aside from the talking cat, much of it is in essence reasonably true. But while Sir Richard (*c*. 1350–1423) is by far the most famous Lord Mayor of London, and unusual in that he held the post four times, the office itself is far older and dates back to one Henry Fitz-Ailwin de Londonestone in 1189.

The notion that the twelfth-century city might be self-governing is said to have been imported from France, the crusading King Richard allowing the merchants and aldermen of London a greater degree of autonomy in return for increased taxes and loans raised by the city's merchants to pay for his foreign adventures.

As a powerful symbol of this greater authority, William Hardel as Lord Mayor in 1215, was the only commoner to sign the Magna Carta. Similarly even now – after nearly 700 Lord Mayors – the process of electing a new man to the post is quite separate from any normal local, regional or national elections. Instead the new Lord Mayor is elected by a show of hands at Guildhall on or near Michaelmas Day, with only aldermen of the City of London being eligible to stand (following an ordinance of 1435) and only liverymen of the City of London being entitled to vote.

That Sir Richard was able to serve multiple terms (1397–8, 1406 and 1419) is by no means unusual, although Lord Mayors are elected for one year only and by custom can no longer serve in consecutive years. Uniquely Hamo de Chigwell held the office a total of six times (1319, 1321–3, 1325 and 1327) while around this same time Nicholas de Farndone and John de Pulteney like Sir Richard were in office four times. The last individual to serve multiple terms served only twice, however: Robert Fowler in 1883 and 1885.

Elected in 1983 Dame Mary Donaldson is so far the only woman to be elected, while Sir David Salomons, Bt MP (1797–1873) – famously the first Jew ever to speak in the House of Commons – was the first Jewish Lord Mayor of London.

Like their predecessors they were charged primarily with representing, supporting and promoting the businesses and citizens of the Square Mile – and so by extension these days the wider British financial services industry.

For this there is no salary although Lord Mayors are handsomely housed in the Mansion House during a year in which they can expect to give at least 800 speeches and to spend almost a third of their time travelling the globe. For twelve months the Lord Mayor is also Chief Magistrate of the City of London, Admiral of the Port of London and Chancellor of City University. And where once tradition called for the holder to be knighted at the start of his term (and given a baronetcy at the end of it) today the reward is to be made a Knight Bachelor but only on retirement.

Where did the **Beatles** give their last **public** performance?

The Fab Four having ceased touring in 1966, they gave their final live performance on the cold, windswept rooftop of the Apple Corps building at 3 Savile Row, W1, on 30 January 1969. Playing started at lunchtime, literally bringing the traffic outside to a complete halt, with George Harrison later claiming that it happened this way only 'because it was much simpler than going anywhere else; also nobody had ever done that, so it would be interesting to see what happened.'

Fortunately much of what he called 'a nice little social study', with Billy Preston joining the four to play the organ and electric piano, was captured on film and saw the light of day in the 1970 fly-on-the-wall documentary *Let It Be*. Unfortunately Harrison's question about what would happen was all too soon answered. The performance was cut short by the police from nearby West End Central, who ordered the playing to stop after just 42 minutes on the grounds that it was disrupting businesses in the adjacent buildings.

In the film, live, al fresco versions of 'Don't Let Me Down', 'I've Got a Feeling', 'Dig a Pony' and 'One After 909' are intercut with candid reactions from pedestrians gathered on the street below. The session also included a brief instrumental version of 'God Save the Queen' while the tape was changed (unfortunately this did not make it into the film) with both Lennon and Starr wearing their wives' coats against the cold.

Aside from its obvious historical significance the occasion is also notable for Paul McCartney ad-libbing new lyrics to 'Get Back', with lines such as 'you've been playing on the roofs again', 'your mummy doesn't like that', and 'that makes her angry . . . she's gonna have you arrested' after the police made their way to the building and attempted to bring the playing to a close. When they succeed in doing this, and to sounds of applause from Apple staff on the roof, John Lennon can be heard saying, 'I'd like to say "thank you" on behalf of the group and ourselves, and I hope we passed the audition.'

The studio tape operator Alan Parsons later referred to the day as 'one of the greatest and most exciting days of my life. To see the Beatles playing together and getting an instant feedback from the people around them, five cameras on the roof, cameras across the road, in the road, it was just unbelievable.' But unfortunately the four were back at no. 3 only a few months later, this time to dissolve the band in what was to be the last time that John, Paul, George and Ringo were ever in the same room together.

Which top **Nazi** was **locked up** in the Tower?

One of the Tower's earliest prisoners was the disgraced Bishop of Durham in 1100, Ranulf Flambard – for such was his name – ensuring his name went down in history by escaping down a rope which had been smuggled into his cell in a casket of wine. Among the last were the Kray twins who were briefly detained there after failing to report for National Service. They did not escape, perhaps because by the 1950s prisoners were no longer allowed to bring intoxicating liquor onto the premises.

Inevitably the Krays' imprisonment in such a place has lent them a certain amount of glamour among their feeble-minded fan club. However, the reality is they were locked up here rather than the local nick only because the regiment to which they had been assigned – 1st Battalion, The Royal Fusiliers (City of London Regiment) – was at that time billeted at the Tower.

Instead the Tower tends rightly to be associated more with royal and noble prisoners than the merely criminal, particularly with those prisoners who were tortured here or held for years on end or suffered the ultimate penalty on the block at Tower Green. Many visitors fail to realise, however, that the Tower's role as a prison and place of execution continued until well into the twentieth century.

In the First World War, for example, no fewer than eleven German spies were lined up and shot outside the Martin Tower. In 1916, as previously noted, the Irish revolutionary Roger Casement was stripped of his knighthood and locked up in the Tower before being removed to Pentonville where he was hanged for treason. And as recently as 1941 another German spy, Corporal Josef Jakobs, was shot to death by a firing squad of eight Scots Guards – the last person to be executed at the Tower.

The last one so far anyway. In fact by this time German spies were generally hanged at Wandsworth in South London, but for some reason an exception was made for Jakobs. (He was also permitted to meet his maker sitting down, having broken one ankle parachuting into Essex carrying British currency, forged papers, a radio and some *knackwurst*.)

Of far greater historical significance than this particular bungler, however, was Hitler's devoted deputy, Rudolf Hess, who spent four days in the Tower in 1941 after becoming the only ranking Nazi to risk putting a foot on British soil during wartime. It's still not entirely clear why he chose to do so, but interesting to note that he too arrived with a broken ankle, sustained after he parachuted from his doomed Messerschmitt Bf 110 onto the Duke of Hamilton's Renfrewshire estate.

During his detention a German-speaking friend of Churchill's, Wg Cdr George Salaman, was put into the same cell at Hess, posing as a captured Luftwaffe officer – several of whom were held at the Tower – in the hope that the high-ranking Hess would let slip some useful intelligence. He never did, perhaps because he had no real beans to spill, and until his return to Germany to stand trial at Nuremburg in 1946 he was officially described as Winston's personal prisoner and known as 'Jonathan'. However, despite a curiously persistent rumour that the wartime PM and 'Jonathan' talked at length at a house at no. 17 Oakleigh Park North in Friern Barnet, it seems highly unlikely the pair ever actually met.

What's the most **dangerous address** in **London**?

If you're a popstar, it's probably worth avoiding 9 Curzon Place, SW1, an architecturally clumsy but otherwise unremarkable apartment block off Park Lane in which was located the modest two-bedroom flat of Harry 'Without You' Nilsson.

In fact Nilsson didn't write his most famous hit at all which was a cover of a Badfinger song whose authors, Pete Ham and Tom Evans, both subsequently committed suicide in a spooky parallel of their own lyric, 'I can't live, if living is without you'. They didn't do it in Flat 12, however, and indeed probably never even set foot in the building, Nilsson having been under the impression that the song was actually one of Lennon and McCartney's.

But the Who's trap-rattler certainly came here, as did one of the Mamas and Papas, both of them eventually leaving Nilsson's fourth-floor flat on a stretcher on their way to join the long list of ill-fated rock 'n' rollers who checked out early while in living or visiting London.

Staying in the flat in the summer of 1974 for a concert at the London Palladium, Ellen Naomi Cohen (better known as Cass Elliot) was the first to go, dying of a heart attack almost certainly brought on by drug use and the prolonged effects of obesity. Just 5ft 5in but 15 stone at the time of her death, the coroner found no proof *post mortem* to support the rumour that the 32-year-old had choked to death on a ham sandwich – but the rumour has proved durable nonetheless.

Four years later Keith Moon came to stay at the same address with girlfriend Annette Walter-Lax. He looked in better shape than Mama Cass but probably wasn't: as 'Moon the Loon' his appetite for wild bingeing on drink and drugs was well-known and clearly taking its toll. Indeed at the time of his death he was being prescribed Heminevrin, a drug used for countering the symptoms of alcohol withdrawal, but with no sense of irony chose to mix it with a bottle of wine or two before falling asleep.

Breakfast the following day was that old late-morning special of thirty-two tablets and a steak, after which Moon was found conked out on the bed and later pronounced DOA at the A&E. His fellow band members had reportedly already accepted that he would probably die prematurely and in this sort of way – one of them, recognising that Moon had tempted fate once too often, said later, 'I think someone looked down and said: okay, that's your ninth life' – and perhaps the only real surprise is that it was prescription drugs which did for him in the end rather than the long and imaginative list of more unorthodox narcotics which he had sampled over the years.

Why does the **Prime Minister** live in **Downing Street**?

For years he didn't, the office of the First Lord of the Treasury – as the earliest Prime Ministers were known – conferring no special benefits on the holder with respect to living accommodation. Instead holders of the position had to make their own living arrangements, and not until 1735 when a certain Mr Chicken surrendered the lease on no. 10 did what was once a small square and is now a fairly humble cul-de-sac become one of the most famous addresses in the world.

The street itself was built in the 1680s by Sir George Downing, Bt (1632–89), a soldier, spymaster and turncoat who was described by Pepys as a 'perfidious rogue' and somehow manoeuvred to serve both Lord Protector Cromwell and King Charles II.

Coming from an entirely respectable Suffolk family – his mother was Lucy Winthrop of Groton, whose brother John was the founder and first governor of Massachusetts – he spent some time locked in the Tower. Once released, and using the fruits of various extortion schemes, he was able to obtain a valuable parcel of land at Whitehall. This was in 1654 but he had to wait nearly thirty years before building his prized 'foure greate houses . . . fronting St James Parke west and east.'

The one we know as no. 10 was originally no. 5, with Sir Robert Walpole the first politician to move here with his family. Abandoning his own palatial home in St James's Square only at the behest of the king, he had at first declined the invitation but then changed his mind on condition that instead of being a gift to him personally no. 10 should 'be & remain for the use & habitation of the first Commissioner of his Majestys Treasury *[sic]*.' Even then it took three years to move Mr Chicken out, together with a neighbour Mr Scroop, and for the properties to be very expensively adapted to their new role.

Thereafter, and for more than 250 years, no. 10 provided the Prime Minister with an official residence – even if it was somewhat modest by the standards of, say, the French or Americans. Nor by any means has every incumbent chosen to live there. For some the accommodation was too modest: Labour's Tony Blair famously prevailed upon his next-door neighbour to swap, the Chancellor of the Exchequer's flat at no. 11 being rather larger. Similarly, while Pitt the Younger reportedly very much enjoyed living at no. 10, for nearly seventy years after his death in 1806 the house was used very rarely and, except for the occasional meetings, it was largely vacant for thirty years.

In part this was because many who were entitled to live there, like Walpole, already had more impressive houses of their own in a better part of town. Often they preferred to lend no. 10 to friends and family members, or even political allies whom they wished to favour. The house was also for a long time in very poor shape structurally, with shallow foundations, decaying chimneys and uneven floorboards making it prone more than occasionally to require very extensive remedial work.

Because of such consideration, in the 1880s, Lord Salisbury very much preferred to commute all the way from Hatfield House in Hertfordshire than live at no. 10; and nearly a century later Harold Wilson was still only pretending to live there, ensuring that he was frequently photographed arriving and leaving but during his second ministry choosing to remain at his much quieter, more private house in Lord North Street behind Westminster Abbey.

In fact only very recently has the true value of the place been recognised, Lady Thatcher stating in its unofficial biography by Christopher Jones – *No. 10 Downing Street, The Story of a House* – 'how much I wish that the public . . . could share with me the feeling of Britain's historic greatness which pervades every nook and cranny of this complicated and meandering old building. All Prime Ministers,' she says, 'are intensely aware that, as tenants and stewards of no. 10 Downing Street, they have in their charge one of the most precious jewels in the nation's heritage.'

Where do **London's** most **famous** next-door **neighbours** live?

If you discount 10 Downing Street and Buckingham Palace as too obvious, the most likely answer must be Cheyne Walk because any celebrity headcount here – of individuals alive or dead, real or fictional – looks certain to beat any other street in the capital.

The Chelsea riverside street takes its name – it's pronounced 'chainy' – from Charles Cheyne, Viscount Newhaven, who bought the manor of Chelsea in 1657 and fathered William

Cheyne who was responsible for planning Cheyne Walk and Cheyne Row between 1708 and 1820. Having never fallen on hard times since then, a list of residents, past and present, would have to include the following. Those shown with an asterisk are commemorated by an official English Heritage blue plaque, of which the Walk has more than any other London street.

Algernon Charles Swinburne*, poet, lived at no. 16.

Cecil Gordon Lawson, the landscape painter, lived at no. 15. So too did engraver Henry Thomas Ryall.

Dante Gabriel Rossetti*, painter and poet, lived at no. 16.

David Lloyd George lived at no. 10.

'Don Saltero', actually James Salter, in the early eighteenth century established a celebrated coffee house at no. 18.

Elizabeth Gaskell*, novelist, was born at no. 93.

George Eliot* (the novelist Mary Anne Evans) spent the last three weeks of her life at no. 4.

Sir Hans Sloane, physician and benefactor, lived at the manor house which was demolished in 1760 having stood on the site now occupied by nos 19–26.

Henry James spent his last years at no. 21.

Hilaire Belloc*, writer and historian, lived at no. 104.

James Henry Leigh Hunt*, painter, lived round the corner at no. 22 Upper Cheyne Row.

Another painter, J.M.W. Turner, died at no. 119 in 1851.

James Abbott McNeill Whistler*, yet another painter, lived at various times at nos 21, 96 and 101.

James Clerk Maxwell lived at no. 41 in the early 1860s and conducted important electromagnetic experiments on the iron railings outside.

John Tweed*, sculptor and friend of Auguste Rodin, lived at no. 108.

Sir Marc and Isambard Kingdom Brunel* lived at no. 98.

Nikolaus Ludwig, Imperial Count von Zinzendorf und Pottendorf, lived at Lindsey House at nos 99–100 in the mid-eighteenth century.

Sir Philip Steer*, painter, lived at no. 109.

Ralph Vaughan Williams lived at no. 13 when he wrote the *Fantasia on a Theme by Thomas Tallis* and *The Lark Ascending*.

Sylvia Pankhurst*, suffragette, lived at no. 120 after leaving university.

Thomas More, saint and former chancellor, lived at Crosby Hall (see below) when it was still at Bishopsgate.

Walter Greaves*, another painter of the Thames, lived at no. 104.

The Walk's more recent residents have included footballer George Best, Mick and 'Keef' of the Rolling Stones, Laurence Olivier and Jill Esmond, the cartoonist Gerald Scarfe and Jane Asher, book collector and cricketing philanthropist John Paul Getty II, the late Paula Yates and two of her men

(Bob Geldof and Michael Hutchence), singer Kylie Minogue, the thriller writer Ken Follett, Sir Jocelyn Stevens of English Heritage, Rupert Allason MP (aka the spy-writer Nigel West), the interior designer John Stefanidis, and Christopher Moran, a successful Lloyds insurance broker who at the time if writing is remodelling as a private house the medieval Crosby Hall, which brick-by-brick was removed here from Bishopsgate in the City in 1908.

Why is **Karl Marx** buried in **London**?

The grave most eagerly sought by visitors to Highgate Cemetery is probably also the most frequently vandalised. The final resting place of Karl Marx (1818–83), it bears cold, mute witness to London's continuing willingness to offer asylum to those whose ideas and philosophies have proved unpopular in the countries of their birth.

Some were fortunate enough to return home eventually, either because the political pendulum eventually swung their way or because they themselves were able to seize power. But Trier-born Marx had no such luck, dying more than three decades before the successful revolution in Tsarist Russia, and

towards the end being in so much pain from haemorrhoids that for a while his dearest wish was that, after he was gone, 'the bourgeoisie will remember my barnacles.'

From the right wing there's not much to rival the author of *The Communist Manifesto* and *Das Kapital*, perhaps only a small stone marking the grave of a Nazi dog in Carlton House Terrace, SW1. (Giro, an alsatian and the beloved pet of the penultimate pre-war German ambassador.) Leftists were clearly welcomed here in greater numbers, together with a number of other radicals and rebels including Mahatma Gandhi, who lived at 20 Baron's Court Road, W14 (not far from Mohammed Ali Jinnah at 35 Russell Road, and indeed Jawaharlal Nehru at 60 Elgin Crescent).

Emperor Napoleon III similarly found a safe billet at 1c King Street, St James's, after his capture in the Franco-Prussian War, his unique status as both a president of France and its last monarch being marked by one of the oldest blue plaques in London (see p. 126).

Elsewhere one finds a home of Giuseppe Mazzini – who was exiled to 183 Gower Street, NW1, following the declaration of his *Apostolato popolare* or Apostleship of the People in 1873 – and in the unlikely setting of Bromley's Crescent Road that of Pyotr Kropotkin. After escaping from St Petersburg's gaunt Peter and Paul Fortress, the celebrated Russian anarchist fled to Switzerland but was told to leave following the assassination of Alexander II.

Yet another political refugee to favour London was the French diplomat Charles Maurice de Talleyrand-Périgord (1754–1838) 1st Sovereign Prince of Beneventum. He put up at 21 Hanover Square and, as a consequence of a severe congenital limp, was even accorded the honour of a special handrail at the Travellers' Club, Pall Mall. After 170 years this is still in place. Finally, at 44 Eaton Square, is a blue plaque to Klemens Wenzel, Prince von Metternich (1773–1859). Vain, self-assured and for a while loudly praised, in the end the sometime Habsburg Austrian Foreign Minister became widely reviled and with the Vienna mob at his door (and baying for his blood after the 1848 Revolution) he fled to Brighton and then London before returning home to die in 1859.

Why isn't there a **Duke of London**?

As the owner of more of it than anyone else – then or now – the logical candidate for the title would have been Hugh Lupus Grosvenor, 1st Duke of Westminster (1825–99) whose central London possessions when his sovereign suggested he be raised from a marquess to a duke included many hundreds of acres in Belgravia, Mayfair and Pimlico.

Already the 3rd Marquess of Westminster, in 1874 he made the unusual request to keep his existing territorial designation, aware perhaps that 'of London' might have sounded too grand for such a serious-minded man as himself. Even the Queen-Empress Victoria, after all, was only the Duke of Lancaster – a subsidiary title and a useful blind when she wished to travel incognito – as a consequence of the sovereign's historic personal possession of the valuable Duchy of Lancaster and its lands.

In fact the only time that the Dukedom of London has been seriously considered was in 1955. Leaving no. 10 Downing Street for the final time, Winston Churchill was famously offered the honour by a grateful queen and country. At this time Prime Ministers were traditionally offered earldoms, and given Churchill's singular contribution, the very considerable promotion is not hard to justify. New dukedoms are rare, however, and had he accepted the honour it would have been the first new one since Fife in 1900, created for the new husband of a grand-daughter of Queen Victoria.

During confidential discussions the wartime leader is believed to have been offered a choice of Dover or London – but in the end chose neither and graciously declined the honour.

Perhaps as the grandson of a duke (born at Blenheim, in his youth he had been Marlborough's heir presumptive) he saw no need for another one. It is also conceivable that, like Mme Chanel who is said to have declined to marry Bend'Or, 2nd Duke of Westminster on the grounds that there were plenty of duchesses but only one Coco – Bend'Or alone created four more by marrying them – he recognised that being Winston Spencer Churchill was distinction enough.

In any event the title was never bestowed, nor is the offer ever likely to be repeated.

6

MONUMENTS

Which is London's **oldest statue**?

Standing in front of the Italianate portico of Holy Trinity Church in Southwark's elegant but little-known late Georgian Trinity Church Square, a weatherbeaten statue thought to be of Alfred the Great is often referred to as the oldest statue in London. It certainly looks venerable, although at something like 600 years old it postdates the famous burner of buns by a good five centuries or more. In fact it's a mere babe-in-arms compared to leading contender for the title, the so-called Sotheby's Sekhmet. A far more ancient black basalt or diorite representation of the Egyptian lion-deity, Sekhmet sits above

the main entrance to the famous auction house at its New Bond Street headquarters but is all too often missed by both visitors and passers-by.

For more than a century the statue has served as the company's unofficial mascot – they maybe prefer the term muse – having arrived at the old Wellington Street premises in the 1800s as part of a large but fairly random collection of Egyptian artefacts which were consigned for sale. In the event the lot was sold for £40 but the buyer failed to collect his very particular purchase so the orphaned goddess was adopted by the staff and removed to 34–5 New Bond Street when Sotheby's came here in 1917.

As well as being the oldest privately owned monument in London – clearly many museums have much older artefacts – Sekhmet's effigy is also by far the capital's oldest outdoor statue, having been carved in Egypt in about 1320 BC.

Today, as I say, few people notice it, but in 1966 it was the subject of a learned article, 'The Bust of Sekhmet' in *Ivory Hammer 4: The Year at Sotheby's & Parke Bernet*, published by Longmans. The two-page article included a contribution from a young Bruce Chatwin, at that time employed as a cataloguer for Sotheby's. He wrote a brief history of the bust, including an investigation of the myths and stories attached to this little-known goddess of war and strife, and as the novelist and travel writer's first published work the piece is today highly collectible.

What was London's **largest** ever **statue**?

In terms of a work which was completed rather than merely planned, the answer is a monumental bronze of Arthur Wellesley, 1st Duke of Wellington. Mounted on his favourite charger Copenhagen surveying the field at Waterloo, it was designed to stand at Hyde Park Corner – in front of the Duke's Apsley House – and remained there for a good few years until the public outcry proved such that it had to be taken down and shipped out to the home counties.

Consuming an incredible 40 tons of bronze, much of which came from captured Napoleonic cannon, 30ft high and a full 26ft from nose to tail, the Duke's likeness is the work of the controversial Matthew Coates Wyatt and his son James. When first completed it was loaded onto a specially-constructed wooden carriage and dragged to Hyde Park Corner by twenty-nine laurel-crowned horses accompanied by 500 guardsmen – whereupon it was apparent immediately that it was built to completely the wrong scale.

Most obviously it was far too big to sit atop Decimus Burton's ceremonial Constitution Arch. But it was also modelled on the wrong horse – the much loved Copenhagen had died a decade earlier – and it quickly became clear that everyone with an opinion to express really hated it.

After a lifetime's distinguished service the Iron Duke warranted an act of *homage* at least equal to Nelson's Column, but for most of the people this wasn't it. Burton went so far as to leave £3,000 in his will to pay for its removal from his arch, while a French visitor on seeing it during a trip to London gleefully declared that he and his countrymen had at last been avenged.

Eventually Queen Victoria agreed that even she considered it to be an eyesore, although to save the old duke's feelings she insisted that it be allowed to stand until after his death. Thereafter it was decided to remove the monster as quickly as was practicable. Shipped out to Round Hill it was duly presented by the Prince of Wales to the Aldershot Division, in the belief that the Army was best placed to appreciate one of its own. In London it was eventually replaced by a statue of Victory, the *Quadriga* by Adrian Jones, which at that time was the largest bronze Europe had ever seen.

The duke's still out in Surrey – ungainly, sculpturally hideous, and so massive that it's hard to credit that at one point someone had proposed something even larger. But actually somewhere someone had: something much, much larger. This was the Greenwich Britannia, conceived a few years earlier – in 1799 – as a celebration of all things British and magnificent, especially our winning ways when it came to fighting wars abroad.

A statue of Britannia Triumphant, surveying the capital from high on Greenwich Hill, its designer declared that his heroine would be an incredible 230ft tall, making it more than twice the height of the Rhodes Colossus and a full 80ft taller than New York's Statue of Liberty. The idea for this 'noblest Monument of National Glory in the world' came from John Flaxman, the Royal Academy's first professor of sculpture as his entry in a competition organised by the Duke of Clarence. Later to accede to the thrown as William IV, Britain's 'sailor king', was keen to see a large naval monument in London to celebrate the wholesale destruction of the French navy at the previous year's Battle of the Nile.

In 1795 the Government had voted to spend some money celebrating British war heroes. Thinking big, Flaxman felt the time was now right for something which would last 'as long as the Trajan Column, the Amphitheatres, or the Pyramids of Egypt [and be] executed in a manner worthy of the grandeur and power of the country.' Such a scheme, he said, would 'ensure the praise and admiration of succeeding ages' and siting it on Greenwich Hill would be the icing on the cake: placing the monument right on the meridian, 'the point from which the world would be measured,' as well as giving it some very considerable additional height.

In the end it all proved too much, and feeling that a rival's pantheon to British art might be a better monument, the sculptor reluctantly withdrew his scheme only for the pantheon scheme also to fail to materialise. Fortunately Flaxman's Britannia didn't go entirely to waste: he used it at a much reduced scale for Nelson's memorial in St Paul's, and in an adjusted form on another to Lord North. Happily William IV and the country got their naval memorial as well, a gigantic free-standing Corinthian column in Trafalgar Square. The man who got to model Nelson – whose likeness stands on top and gazes down Whitehall – was a student of Flaxman's called Edward Hodges Bailey.

Where are London's **strangest statues**?

Despite suffering the ignominy *post mortem* of having his likeness banished from London, the Duke of Wellington can at least take comfort from the fact that there are several more commemorative statues to him around the capital. These include a replacement bronze of himself at Hyde Park Corner – correctly seated on Copenhagen, and sensibly a good deal smaller – with a stone carving at the Royal Arsenal in Woolwich, and another equestrian bronze outside the Royal Exchange in the City.

In fact Wellington is the only person, royalty included, to have two equestrian statues to him in London, although even he can't match the unique distinction of Dame Louisa Aldrich-Blake in Tavistock Square. One of several statue-peculiarities around the capital, the pioneering woman surgeon is for some reason depicted twice on the same monument, a large column designed by Sir Edwin Lutyens.

At Heathrow a likeness of transatlantic aviators Sir John Alcock and Sir Arthur Brown is equally unusual in that they are depicted in full flying rig, while that of Lord Byron in Hamilton Gardens, W1, is distinguished by being so unlike its subject that his friend Edward Trelawny reportedly failed to recognise it as being of Byron.

The statue of Florence Nightingale which stands on the north terrace of St Thomas's Hospital is something of an oddity too: it's actually a plastic-composite copy of the bronze original which was stolen in 1970 and has never been recovered. The memorial to another hero, Franklin D. Roosevelt in Grosvenor Square, has a far happier tale to tell, however, the lifesize bronze which his widow unveiled in 1948 being funded by more than 200,000 public donations of less than five shillings each – all of them pledged and paid on a single day.

In Waterlow Park off Highgate Hill the statue of Sir Sidney Waterlow Bt, MP is almost certainly the first statue ever to depict a man with an umbrella (he's also holding a key, signifying his generosity in giving the park to the people) but far stranger is the sixteenth-century carving in Henry VII Chapel at Westminster Abbey of St Matthew reading a book. Described in Vincent Ilardi's book *Renaissance Vision from Spectacles to Telescopes*, the statue is almost certainly the first ever to show somebody wearing a pair of glasses. The first with a violin is similarly that of Wolfgang Amadeus Mozart, shown as a young child in Orange Square, SW1, close to Ebury Street where for a while he lived (and where at the age of eight he composed his first symphony).

As for the most obscure subject for a statue, it's a toss-up between a tenth-century Ukranian saint and an eighteenth-century Liverpool MP. The first, Vladimir Svyatoslavich the Great, son of Sviatoslav I of Kiev and otherwise known as Volodymyr, has somehow landed on the corner of Holland Park and Holland Park Avenue. Then in Pimlico Gardens we have the toga-wearing William Huskisson, a man whose sole distinction seems to be that he was the first man ever to be knocked down and killed by a train. Sir Osbert Sitwell nicknamed it, 'Boredom rising from the Bath' – which seems to say it all.

Why was **Ben Jonson** buried **standing up**?

The actor and dramatist Ben Jonson (1572–1637) managed to get one of the much-prized plots close to Poets' Corner in Westminster Abbey – plenty of equally eminent men and women who apply don't make it – but, bizarrely, was buried standing up, having agreed to a grave just 18in square. It's likely he did this because as his death approached he was living in very considerably reduced circumstances, further proof of which can be seen in the inscription, *O Rare Ben Johnson*, in which his name was casually misspelt by the calibre of stonemason you get stuck with if, like Jonson, you can afford to pay only eighteen pence to get the job done.

As *Kapellmeister* to the Elector of Hanover – later King George I – George Frederick Handel fared slightly better. When it came to sculpting his effigy for the abbey, Louis-François Roubillac agreed that the deceased had a good ear for music but refused to sculpt his real ones which he thought were simply too ugly to be rendered into marble. His solution, besides leaving the right ear off completely, was to model a new left one from the (he thought) more delicate lugs of a certain Miss Rich. (Sir Edwin Landseer famously had to do something similar in Trafalgar Square. When the lion he'd been lent as a model sickened and died, the smell of it decomposing was reportedly so bad that the paws for the lions at the foot of Nelson's Column were instead copied from those of a domestic moggy.)

Finally, before leaving the abbey, take a peep at the wax model of Frances Stuart (1648–1702), the wife of the 3rd Duke of Richmond and 6th of Lennox. Having posed as Britannia for a number of coins issued during the reign of Charles II – she remained his mistress for many years, despite being disfigured by

smallpox – her lifesize effigy is dressed in her actual coronation robes and accompanied by what is almost certainly the oldest stuffed bird in the country, her much loved African Grey.

Who is the **Unknown Warrior**?

Although he was recently voted no. 76 in a nationwide poll of the 100 Greatest Britons of all time, the reality is that no-one knows beyond the fact that he was killed on a European battlefield at some point during the First World War. Precisely which battlefield has never been revealed, the secret being deliberately maintained in order that his tomb might serve as a universal symbol for all of the unknown dead, regardless of where or when they fell.

The idea for such a thing was first mooted in 1916 by the Revd David Railton MC, a vicar from Kent. Serving as an army chaplain on the Western Front, and seeing a grave in a back garden at Armentières marked by a rough cross and bearing the pencil-written legend 'An Unknown British Soldier', he wrote to the Dean of Westminster in 1920 suggesting that one such be buried with due reverence 'among the kings'.

Though not without opposition from those who didn't wish to reopen old wounds – the king in particular found the notion distasteful – his idea for a Tomb of the Unknown Warrior was eventually taken up by the Prime Minister David Lloyd George and following an emotional response from the public, arrangements were placed in the hands of Britain's great ceremonial impressario, Earl Curzon of Kedleston.

In November of that year four bodies draped with Union flags were removed to the chapel at Ste Pol near Arras in France. On the night of the 7th one of these was selected at random by Brigadier General L.J. Wyatt, accompanied by Lieutenant Colonel E.A.S. Gell of the Directorate of Graves Registration and Enquiries. Placed in a simple pine coffin with a plaque declaring 'A British Warrior who fell in the Great War', the body was transferred under guard the following afternoon to the castle library at Boulogne Citadel where a company from the French 8th Infantry Regiment stood vigil overnight.

On 9 November two undertakers arrived and placed the coffin in a casket of oak timbers from Hampton Court Palace, to which was attached a medieval crusader's sword chosen by George V personally from the Royal Collection. This was surmounted by an iron shield bearing the inscription 'A British Warrior who fell in the Great War 1914–1918 for King and Country'.

Before its departure for England, Marshal Foch saluted the casket as it was carried up the gangway of the destroyer, HMS *Verdun* and piped aboard with an admiral's call. Slipping anchor just before noon, and escorted by six battleships, the casket received a 19-gun field marshal's salute as it passed Dover Castle. Once landed it was taken to Victoria station, arriving at platform 8 at 8.32 p.m. and remaining there for the night of the 10th. (A plaque nearby now records this fact.)

On the morning of 11 November 1920 – Armistice Day – the casket was loaded onto a gun carriage of the Royal Horse Artillery and drawn by six horses through immense and silent crowds. As it passed Whitehall the new Cenotaph was formally unveiled by the king, the cortège then making its way to Westminster Abbey followed by the His Majesty, the royal family and various ministers of state.

After being borne into the West Nave of the abbey where it was flanked by a guard of honour of one hundred recipients of the Victoria Cross, the coffin was interred in the far western end of the nave, only a few feet from the entrance, with soil from each of the main battlefields and a cap of black Belgian marble. Today it is the only tombstone in the abbey on which one is forbidden to walk. It bears the following inscription, composed by Bishop Ryle, Dean of Westminster, and engraved with brass melted down from wartime ammunition:

> BENEATH THIS STONE RESTS THE BODY
> OF A BRITISH WARRIOR
> UNKNOWN BY NAME OR RANK
> BROUGHT FROM FRANCE TO LIE AMONG
> THE MOST ILLUSTRIOUS OF THE LAND
> AND BURIED HERE ON ARMISTICE DAY
> 11 NOV: 1920, IN THE PRESENCE OF
> HIS MAJESTY KING GEORGE V
> HIS MINISTERS OF STATE
> THE CHIEFS OF HIS FORCES
> AND A VAST CONCOURSE OF THE NATION
> THUS ARE COMMEMORATED THE MANY
> MULTITUDES WHO DURING THE GREAT
> WAR OF 1914 – 1918 GAVE THE MOST THAT
> MAN CAN GIVE LIFE ITSELF
> FOR GOD
> FOR KING AND COUNTRY
> FOR LOVED ONES HOME AND EMPIRE
> FOR THE SACRED CAUSE OF JUSTICE AND
> THE FREEDOM OF THE WORLD
> THEY BURIED HIM AMONG THE KINGS BECAUSE HE
> HAD DONE GOOD TOWARD GOD AND TOWARD
> HIS HOUSE

When Lady Elizabeth Bowes-Lyon married the future King George VI on 26 April 1923, she laid her bouquet at the tomb on her way into the abbey, a gesture which has since been copied by every royal bride married at the abbey. Today the bell of the *Verdun* still hangs close to the tomb, and it's also good to know that when the Nazi idealogue Alfred Rosenberg visited Britain on a diplomatic mission in 1933 and laid a wreath with a Swastika on it, an old soldier promptly snatched it off and threw it into the Thames.

Why is it said that **pin-ups** underpin **Cleopatra's Needle**?

With its twin standing in New York's Central Park, the red granite obelisk on the Embankment known as Cleopatra's Needle has no genuine connection with the famous queen. Having been quarried near Aswan and erected in the city of Heliopolis on the orders of Thutmose III in about 1450 BC, it actually predates Cleo by a good 1,400 years.

For London the story starts more than 3,200 years later, in 1819 when it was presented by the Ottoman Muhammad Ali Pasha al-Mas'ud ibn Agha, Turkish Viceroy of Egypt and Sudan. He made the presentation in commemoration of the twin victories of Lord Nelson at the Battle of the Nile and of Sir Ralph Abercromby at the Battle of Alexandria.

Unfortunately, the donor having made no allowance for transporting it here, his gift remained in Alexandria for the next half-century until a sponsor was found in the person of the distinguished anatomist Sir William James Erasmus Wilson. In 1877, at a cost put at £10,000, the stone was carefully dug out of the sand (in which it had lain for at least two millennia) encased in a great iron cylinder built for the purpose and despatched to London in the tow of the 1,329-ton SS *Olga*.

The voyage was a near-total disaster, with six men dying during a storm in the Bay of Biscay and the cylinder drifting out of control for several days before being rescued by the Glasgow steamer *Fitzmaurice*. With order restored it was eventually towed home and up the Thames by the paddle-tug *Anglia* under the command of one Captain Glue.

Safely landed, it was then erected on the Victoria Embankment between two Victorian bronze sphinxes, it being noticed only later that these had been installed the wrong way round so that they appear to be gazing at the obelisk rather than guarding it. Indeed, perhaps because of this careless oversight, the ensemble was badly damaged by enemy action on 4 September 1917, a 110lb bomb falling on a passing tram and leaving a number of shrapnel wounds which are still visible on the right-hand sphinx.

This later damage notwithstanding, the safe if absurdly delayed arrival of Muhammad Ali's gift was marked by the placing of a sealed container in the plinth on which it was intended to stand. The Americans like to think they invented the concept of such a 'time capsule' for the 1939 New York World's Fair, but beneath Cleopatra's Needle is proof that we Brits got there first. That said, the contents are eccentric to say the least. Together with a copy of *Whitaker's Almanack* for 1878, put aside for future generations to find were ten daily newspapers and a copy of *Bradshaw's Railway Guide*, a portrait of Queen Victoria, not one but several different copies of the Bible, a full set of British coins and an Indian rupee, a version of the story told above, a shilling razor and some hairpins, children's toys, one of the jacks which had been used to raise the Needle up in the first place, a box of cigars, several pipes and – most unexpectedly of all, from the staid Victorians – a set of twelve photographs depicting the dozen greatest beauties of the day.

Who is **Eros**?

A fairly minor deity, as the Greek equivalent of Cupid, the mythical god of love, Eros is a long way from being the most obvious choice for a statue in central London – especially as Piccadilly Circus, while long a popular place for a rendezvous, could hardly be described as one of the city's more romantic locations. In fact the clue to his being here is in the name of the adjacent street, Shaftesbury Avenue, and the fact that the monument should more correctly be called the Shaftesbury Memorial Fountain.

Most obviously this is because it was created to commemorate the life and achievements of a noted Victorian benefactor and leading anti-slavery campaigner, the 7th Earl of Shaftesbury. The figure of a male archer is also meant to represent the Angel of Christian Charity – somewhat closer to Lord Shaftesbury's own interests – rather than an ancient, pagan god.

Paid for by public subscription, and sculpted by Alfred Gilbert, the statue is noteworthy as the first in London to be cast in aluminium instead of bronze. The model for the sculpture was a 16-year-old boy, Gilbert's Italian studio assistant Angelo Colarossi, who had earlier posed for another work depicting not Eros but his twin Anteros. Its nakedness aroused considerable controversy when it was unveiled by the Duke of Westminster in 1893.

It was unfortunate too that the sculptor declined to attend the ceremony, being still furious at the continual interference to which he had been subjected by members of the committee responsible for commissioning the work. Nor was it much of a success as a fountain, with one of a quartet of chained drinking cups – almost certainly the one from which the duchess had taken a first draught – being stolen within a couple of days while the bowl of the fountain was so small that passers-by were drenched when the waterworks were switched on.

These niggles aside, the fountain has been moved several times since then, most recently when the area to the south was pedestrianised. It also spent the war years in protective custody at Egham in Surrey, and from 1922 to 1931 was removed to Embankment Gardens while Piccadilly Underground station was being excavated down below. Moving it had called for considerable care, Gilbert having very deliberately aligned the archer's arrow towards Wimborne St Giles, Shaftesbury's Dorset seat, while directing it downwards to make a slightly painful pun on the earl's name with the *shaft* being *buried*.

Who has the **most blue plaques** in London?

A London initiative, but one since copied around the world, the blue plaque scheme was first proposed in 1866 by the reforming politician William Ewart. Thirty years earlier he had successfully campaigned to abolish the punishment of hanging in chains, and the first plaque, which was actually chocolate-brown, was erected in 1867 to Lord Byron in Holles Street, Westminster.

Unfortunately the building in which he lived was later demolished so that today the two oldest plaques (dating from 1875) commemorate the poet John Dryden in Soho and Emperor Napoleon III in St James's. The latter was accorded the genuinely unique honour of a plaque while still alive, the rule for everyone else being that at least twenty years must have passed since the candidate's death or a century since their birth.

The first woman to get a plaque was the novelist Fanny Burney (1752–1840) in Bolton Street, W1, with cricketer W.G. Grace the first sportsman to be honoured (in SE9). On North Common Road, Ealing, the seven-times Wimbledon champion Dorothea Lambert Chambers (1878–1960) was likewise the first sportswoman, at a time when literary types and politicians were more likely to be noticed. The aforementioned time rule also mitigates against any younger or more recent celebrities being included, although in 1997 a plaque was installed on the façade of the house adjacent to Handel's in Brook Street, Mayfair. It reads 'Jimi Hendrix 1942–70 Guitarist and Songwriter Lived Here 1968–69'.

Hendrix was clearly in residence only relatively briefly, and at Powis Road, E3, Mahatma Gandhi is recorded as having only 'stayed', his greater historical significance and international stature presumably compensating for the brevity. Unusually the Mahatma is honoured by a second plaque, in Barons Court where he lived as a law student, although such duplication is still relatively rare.

Of the other 'multiples' the Statesmen Sir Joseph Chamberlain has two – in Camberwell Grove, and Highbury Place, N5 – as indeed does Samuel Taylor-Coleridge. Confusingly Samuel

Coleridge-Taylor gets one too, the author of the 'Song of Hiawatha' having lived in South Norwood. Another Samuel, Pepys, has one at no. 12 Buckingham Street, Strand, and then a second next door at no. 14.

The anti-slavery campaigner William Wilberforce meanwhile gets no fewer than three plaques – having lived at Broomwood Road, SW11, worshipped at Holy Trinity Church, Clapham Common, and died at Cadogan Place, SW1. So too does Lord Palmerston, also William Makepeace Thackeray, in Palace Green and Young Street (W8) and at 36 Onslow Square, SW7. Dante Gabriel Rossetti's progress across London is similarly mapped by various plaques as he moved from Hallam Street, W1, to Red Lion Square in Bloomsbury before ending up at Cheyne Walk, Chelsea. Churchill, curiously, warrants just the one however – perhaps by 1974 they'd finally tightened up the rules – as does their inventor, William Ewart, at 16 Eaton Place, SW1.

7

SPORT & LEISURE

Which are the **10 oldest football clubs** in London?

1879	Fulham
1881	Leyton Orient
1882	Tottenham Hotspur
1882	Barnet
1885	Millwall
1886	Queens Park Rangers
1886	Arsenal
1889	Brentford
1889	Wimbledon
1895	West Ham

There's nothing new about football, with the Greeks, Romans and ancient Chinese certainly busy kicking balls around long before we did. The Romans called it *harpastum*, a game which is thought to have been adapted from the Greek *episkyros* or *phaininda*. Similarly from China in the first century BC comes documentary evidence of something called *cuju* (literally 'kick-ball') which later spread to Japan and Korea where it was known as *kemari* and *chuk-guk* respectively.

None of this stops fans in this country claiming the game as their own, however, although occasionally the better informed among them are at least generous enough to acknowledge that some elements of the game were imported by intrepid

English explorers. Men such as John Davis, perhaps, who played a form of it with the eskimaux of Greenland, and William Strachey who observed Native Americans at play as early as 1610. Robert Brough-Smyth's *The Aborigines of Victoria* (1878) also cites the example nearly forty years earlier of Aboriginal men kicking around with their chums using an inflated possum skin.

Certainly if the rest of the world was playing it so long before we were it would explain why we lose so often, but in any event it was relatively late arriving in London with Fulham the first club to be established here. In 1879 it converted from an amateur church side – then called St Andrews – before turning pro a few years later.

Such humble origins were hardly unusual. Leyton Orient broke out from a theological college cricket club, becoming the 'Os' at the suggestion of a player whose daytime job was with the Orient Shipping Line. Tottenham Hotspur was formed by boys from the local grammar school. Millwall originally drew its players from the workforce at a jam factory on the Isle of Dogs, with Arsenal another works team, based at Woolwich Arsenal (hence the 'Gunners' nickname). Finally Brentford was an offshoot of a Thames rowing club whose members fancied trying something new and only narrowly avoiding becoming a rugby club instead.

These early formations were obviously amateur, and indeed it wasn't until the early twentieth century that big business finally cut in, doing so at Stamford Bridge where a couple of entrepreneurs bought an athletics stadium before they even had a team to play in it. Eventually forced to found their own team, they did so only because the squad at Fulham declined their invitation to jump ship and move across. Bizarrely the new Chelsea FC was allowed to join the new Football League before they had played even a single game – presumably because, then as now, money talks louder than anything else when it comes to sport.

Where might one have found a **church** full of **prizefighters**?

Today the Ring on Blackfriars Road is a pub, the original building having been all but destroyed by enemy action after two direct hits from the Luftwaffe. That it was is something of a disaster, for what had by then become London's premier boxing arena was a quite extraordinary building, originally built as the Surrey Chapel by a charismatic if somewhat eccentric evangelical by the name of Rowland Hill (1744–1833).

The son of another equally eccentric Rowland Hill – creator of Shropshire's wonderful, folly-strewn Hawkstone Park, and not to be confused with yet another who invented the Penny Post – the Old Etonian was six times refused ordination by six different bishops and so decided to establish his own chapel at Blackfriars in 1783. He did so on the firm understanding that the chapel would not align itself to the theological teachings of any particular denomination, and was inspired to design a large and attractive polygon with a circular interior to deny the devil any corners in which to hide.

Hill was by no means a crank however, and was soon attracting vast congregations, sometimes preaching to them himself and at other times inviting along anyone else who wished to have a go. He also founded and in its early days chaired the Religious Tract Society, established London's first Sunday School, actively promoted the distribution of the Bible to the poor of many nations, and as a friend of Dr Edward Jenner became a fervent advocate of inoculation against smallpox. At a time when this was a major killer a leading physician of the day wrote to him saying, 'by your example, and perhaps next to Jenner, [you] have been the means of saving more lives than any other individual'.

Hill's chapel survived his death in 1833 and he was buried beneath the pulpit. By 1859 it was decided not to renew the lease, however, and the organisation moved to the corner of Westminster Bridge Road and Kennington Park Road, taking

Hill's body with them for reburial in what became the new Lincoln Memorial Tower. The original chapel for a while fell into disrepair and was used for a variety of commercial purposes before being adapted to the needs of boxing promoters in about 1910.

This time it was the brainchild of one Dick Burge, a former British lightweight champion who wished to provide top-class boxing at prices 'the working class public could afford'. For a few years the place was quite a success too, but by the 1930s the general industrial depression took its toll on ticket sales along with increasing competition from newer, better venues and other working-class attractions such as dog tracks. By 1942 with destruction raining down on London, few cared about its future, and today the site of Hill's pioneering chapel is occupied by an award-winning office development called Palestra, a modest allusion to the location's former sporting heritage.

How many times has **London** hosted the **Olympics**?

More than its fair share, one would say, with the 2012 Olympics and 2012 Paralympics the third and fourth occasions that the capital has hosted the games. That's more than anyone else in the modern era – prior to which, of course, it was always the turn of Greece – although this has been more by luck or ill-luck than anything more persuasive.

In 1908, for example, the Games of the IV Olympiad had been scheduled to take place in Rome until the eruption of Mount Vesuvius on 7 April 1906 forced the Italian Government to direct what funds it had toward more pressing matters. London stepped in as a last-minute replacement, hosting an impressive 110 events which saw Britain securing the top slot at the White City Stadium with around three times as many medals as the second-placed team from the USA.

Bizarrely the events included something called 'Motor Boating, Open Class', the first and indeed last time that artificial power has made an appearance at the Olympics. (The winner was a Frenchman who was the only competitor who managed to complete the course.) Britain did rather better in the tug-of-war, winning gold, silver and bronze by fielding three different teams from the Metropolitan, City of London and Liverpool police forces. America withdrew in disgust, citing the Liverpudlians' use of 'illegal boots', but at least got to see the Aussies completely thrash the home team at rugby – the score was 32–3 – thereby setting a pattern which remained in force for much of the next 100 years.

The 1944 event was ours officially, the Games of the XIII Olympiad being awarded to London in 1939 only to be cancelled immediately afterwards when Germany marched into Poland.

With Europe soon in flames, a group of Polish PoWs in the Woldenberg camp staged their own on what would otherwise have been the 50th anniversary of the Modern Olympiad. While the Poles flew an Olympic flag made from bedding,

the IOC HQ in Lausanne promised London another chance providing it didn't lose the war.

Accordingly four years later, in 1948, athletes from fifty-nine nations gathered in London for the Games of the XIV Olympiad. Designed to be a great show of international solidarity, it nevertheless deliberately excluded sportsmen and women from Germany and Japan. With 136 different events, and no money to build from scratch, Wembley took centre stage with numerous other facilities being roped in to help out, including the Empress Hall at Earl's Court, part of the garrison at Aldershot, and a staff sports club owned by the Lyon's Corner House chain at Sudbury. This time Britain came twelfth overall – with just 23 medals to the Americans' 84 – and after winning a gold medal a Czech gymnast called Marie Provaznikova refused to go home thereby becoming the first person ever to defect during the games.

Where is London's **largest** swimming **pool**?

Famously 'a little bit of seaside in the city', open-air swimming has a long history in London with the Serpentine Swimming

Club established as long ago as 1864 – members of the Peter Pan Club still meet for a dip every Christmas morning – and Hampstead and Highgate ponds attracting many hundreds of dippers who like to swim among the fish and weeds.

Fortunately for those who find so-called wild swimming a tad too wild, the capital also has a number of historic lidos, the oldest of which is at Tooting Bec, SW16. This opened on 28 July 1906 as the 'Tooting Bathing-Lake', making it not just the oldest purpose-built open-air pool in London but also, after more than 100 years, the largest swimming pool in the UK and at 300ft by 100ft one of the largest in the whole of Europe.

Containing a million gallons of water, and for many years strictly segregated when it came to male and female bathers, it was originally conceived by the Revd John Hendry Anderson, Rector of Tooting, as a means of providing work for the local unemployed digging the hole. Once finished, as the Mayor of Wandsworth put it, the borough's new cold-water pool would prove ideal 'as a means of affording pleasure, stimulating health and warding off disease.'

In the 1930s to afford its users even greater pleasure a café was built on the site by the London County Council Parks Department. Male and female swimmers were at last allowed to frolic in the water at the same time, and the old fashioned 'dressing sheds' were adapted to provide individual cubicles with doors and seats. These are still there today, their alternating bright blue, red, yellow, and green doors and the contrasting turquoise of the pool sides making the lido a popular location for filming and photo shoots.

While many rival lidos have closed over the years, London remains reasonably well served with similar pools still open at Brockwell Park, Charlton, Ealing (actually privately owned), Hampton, London Fields, at the King's Head pub in Epping Forest and the Oasis in Holborn, on Parliament Hill, at Richmond and by the Serpentine. None quite matches the glories of Tooting, but hopes are high for a revival with plans for a new one at Finchley, and even talk of a 'floating lido' somewhere on the Thames.

Which is London's **oldest theatre**?

With more mainstream theatres than any other city in the world – forty or so in the West End alone – London also started earlier than most with the first playhouse opening in Shoreditch in 1576. Called the Theatre, and owned by actor James Burbage, it lasted just twenty-one years but upon its demolition the timbers were reused to build Shakespeare's famous 'Wooden O', the Globe, at which Burbage's son Richard was one of the bard's early shareholders.

This sort of unroofed, polygonal structure was very much the norm for theatres at this time. So too was its location on the Southwark shore of the Thames, where other theatres such as the Rose sprang up in the so-called Liberty of the Clink where the writ of the all powerful City didn't run. Technically held under the Bishopric of Winchester's rather loose authority, the area fast became the principal entertainment district for London (also its red-light district) with dramatic arts of all kinds being considered at this time far from respectable.

Because of this the wholesale move to the West End, and the switch to the more familiar horseshoe-shaped auditorium and proscenium arch, had to wait until the seventeenth century, the change coming in 1662, just two years after the Restoration. In that year, and in marked contrast to the dour Cromwell, the theatre-loving Charles II granted a patent or licence to Thomas Killgrew and a band of entertainers called 'The King's Servants' for a new theatre on Drury Lane in Covent Garden.

Technically part of the Royal Household and so required to wear a livery of gold and scarlet, the new troupe operated from the grandly titled but initially quite modest premises of the new 700-seat Theatre Royal. (It was here, from the Royal Box, that the king is said to have fallen for Nell Gwynn who made her debut in John Dryden's *The Indian Queen*.)

Today's theatre, however, while old, is very much not the original. This was razed to the ground in 1672, Christopher Wren designing a replacement whose foundations can still be detected beneath the stage. Unfortunately this fell into decline following the deaths of Killigrew and his king, being later revived through the efforts of the actor-manager Thomas Doggett and others (see p. 50) in the early 1700s. This second building was also the setting for a celebrated performance of *The Merchant of Venice* said to have been so moving that George II was unable to sleep either during the performance (as he sometimes did) or indeed for some while afterwards.

Over the years other actor-managers who took the reins at the theatre included David Garrick (see overleaf) and Richard Brinsley Sheridan who besides debuting his own *School for Scandal* here, placed the equally celebrated Mrs Sarah Siddons in the role of Lady Macbeth. In 1794 the theatre was again rebuilt, only to burn down again in 1809 with Sheridan watching from the sidelines, glass in hand, and famously protesting that a man should be permitted 'a drink by his own fireside'. Its replacement was designed by Benjamin Wyatt in 1812 who modelled it on the elegant neo-Classical Grand Theatre at Bordeaux.

Who was **David Garrick?**

With a Garrick Theatre, a Garrick Club, a Garrick Brasserie, a Garrick Street, a Grade I-listed Garrick Villa on the river, a Garrick House not far away, and even an island in the Thames which bears his name, it seems fair to ask why this one long-dead actor-manager should have captured the imagination so much more than all the others.

A friend and pupil of the Lichfield lexicographer Dr Johnson, David Garrick's principal claim as an actor is to have brought to the stage a more realistic, less dramatic style of acting at a time when performances would more commonly have been larger and much more bombastic. A small man at 5ft 4in, and with a relatively soft voice, his naturalistic style proved very popular with audiences and in a sense is still with us today.

Restoring, in the words of one biographer, 'nature, ease, simplicity and genuine humour' to the stage, it was moreover so much a departure from the prevailing style that one contemporary was moved to observe that, 'if this young fellow be right, then we have been *all* wrong.' Garrick himself similarly recorded that a noted patron of the arts, Lord Lyttleton, once 'told me he never knew what acting was till I appeared.'

This new way of acting was quickly adopted by others, and his twenty-nine-year tenure of the aforementioned Theatre Royal genuinely transformed it into one of the greatest playhouses anywhere in Europe. Indeed such was his status and personal prestige when he died in 1779 that the sixty-two-year-old was accorded the distinction of being the first actor ever to buried in Westminster Abbey. (The second was Laurence Olivier, more than two centuries later.)

When the Garrick Club was founded in 1831, by a group of literary sorts under the patronage of HRH the Duke of Sussex, it was intended as a place where 'actors and men of refinement and education might meet on equal terms [and where] patrons of the drama and its professors were to be brought together,' to enjoy 'easy intercourse . . . between artists and patrons.' As the leading Shakespearian actor of his day, Garrick must have seemed the obvious man to lend his name to the new establishment although today only a tiny minority of members work as actors. (Mind you, that was probably always the case: the great Henry Irving was blackballed in the early days, while a duke, five marquesses, half a dozen earls and twice as many barons were cheerfully brought on board.)

Strictly speaking Garrick Street is named after the club not the man, the members with a characteristic lack of reticence having lobbied hard to change the name of what had hitherto been called New King Street. However, when the Garrick Theatre opened in 1889 it certainly took its name from the actor, while Garrick House and Garrick Villa in Hampton are so called because he bought them, one for himself and one for his nephew, with his Viennese widow living as a recluse in the latter for more than forty years. Finally there is Garrick's Ait, formerly known as Shank's Eyot, and sitting midstream on the Thames close to the two houses. It can only be reached by boat, but is nevertheless inhabited with approximately twenty houses all told.

Who invented the **Tube Challenge**?

Requiring competitors to visit every one of the more than 270 stations on the London Underground in the shortest possible time – it's much harder than it sounds – the Tube Challenge is distinguished from the usual sort of London-based lunacy by being listed in and officially vetted by the *Guinness Book of World Records*.

At the time of writing the record stands at 18 hrs, 35 mins, 38 seconds, an improvement of just five seconds over the previous record which if nothing else gives one some indication as to how hard the challenge is and how ferocious the competition.

The challenge itself was invented back in June 1959 when, armed with little more than a Thermos and a copy of Harry Beck's iconic Tube map, R.J. Lewis and D.R. Longley set out to cover the entire Tube network in a single day. At that time there were 277 stations – with lines stretching deep into rural Essex and Bucks – although the total has had to be adjusted many times over the decades with station closures, new lines opening and so forth.

Raising a small fortune for charity, Robert Robinson is the undisputed king of the challenge, having made more than fifty attempts between 1979 and 2000. He has also introduced his sons to the sport at the ages of eight and ten, thereby making them the youngest ever to complete the course.

Most of their rivals have been put off doing it more than once by the sheer demands made on them in terms of planning, strategy and stamina. They might prefer instead a number of smaller, less rigorous challenges, such as the far simpler Zone 1 Challenge, the self-explanatory Circle Line Pub Crawl, the All-Lines Challenge – apparently it's possible to travel on all eleven in barely more than half an hour – and finally, for District Line commuters only, the sprint event which is held on the second

Monday of April every year and which sees a variety of City types jumping off the train at South Ken and sprinting down the road in an attempt to board the same train before it pulls out of Fulham Broadway.

For most challengers, however, the original competition remains the best – and is likely to remain so, being not just so much more challenging but also a living thing which changes year on year as lines shrink and grow and stations open and close.

In the 1960s, for example, the challenge included those stations on the semi-rural Epping–Ongar branch of the Central Line, but there were no Victoria or Jubilee lines to consider and the Piccadilly Line did not yet extend as far as Heathrow.

A decade later the Victoria Line was partly completed, missing only the section between Victoria and Brixton, and by 1975 the Piccadilly Line went as far as Hatton Cross but the Northern Line lost two stations, Drayton Park and Essex Road. Heathrow joined up two years later, but the airport loop was not completed until the mid-1980s.

Meanwhile, out in Essex, Blake Hall closed in the autumn of 1981, with the service between Epping and Ongar reduced to peak hours only, posing all sorts of problems for challengers. Fortunately services ended between Watford Junction and Harrow & Wealdstone, thereby reducing the number of stations by half a dozen.

In 1992, on the Northern Line, Mornington Crescent closed for a total of six years, as did the whole of the Ongar Line and Aldwych station apparently for good. The East London Line also disappeared for a while, being replaced by a bus service from 1995 to 1998. Comparisons between one year and the next are thus the stuff of statisticians' nightmares, but the challengers seem to love it.

Why isn't **Champagne** called **London**?

Although London Buns have been around for so long no-one knows quite where they came from, the capital has never been short of recipes it can call its own. Chelsea Buns, for example, were first made in the seventeenth century at the corner of Lower Sloane Street and Pimlico Road. (You can tell a true one by its edges which should be white and fluffy to show where it was separated from its neigbours.) Maids of Honour likewise take their name from a famous row of terraced houses in Richmond, built for ladies-in-waiting to the former Caroline of Brandenburg-Anspach, wife of George II.

The Salisbury steak, a kind of local beefburger, was devised by a doctor of that name in a patriotic attempt between the wars to banish the unsavoury Germanic associations of the 'hamburger', while Omelette Arnold Bennett and Pêche Melba were created at the Savoy Hotel for the respectively named novelist and opera singer. Finally there is the sandwich: named after the first man to eat one of them. John Montagu, 4th Earl of Sandwich, was too busy at the gaming tables of White's to order a proper supper (or with his ministerial boxes at the Admiralty, depending on whom you ask) and so asked for something simple that he could readily eat with one hand.

But what London really lacks is a local drink. There's the Buck's Fizz, which is popularly but not entirely convincingly said to have been created by a barman at the gentlemen's club of that name in Clifford Street. And of course London Dry Gin as well, although the problem here is that the stuff doesn't even have to be made in London to qualify. (In recent times only Beefeater has been, in the shadow of the Kennington Oval.) The name is a bit of a giveaway too, being derived from the old French, *genevre*, meaning juniper with its earliest origins found not here but in the Netherlands where the Dutch first distilled grain and flavoured it with piquant berries and other aromatic botanicals.

All of which is why, especially now that English wine-growers are doing so fantastically well (and climate change looks set to make English vineyards even better) it's perhaps time to mount a campaign to regain ownership of what is arguably the most celebrated drink in the world.

Across the Channel they'll tell you the famous sparkling wine was the creation of one of a Benedictine monk called Dom Pierre Pérignon (1638–1715), who from 1668 was employed as a cellarman at the Abbey of Hautvillers near Épernay. His is a romantic tale but unlikely to be true – not least because in his lifetime the wines of Champagne were predominantly still and red – which is why there's an increasingly strong case to be made for his English rival.

It's true that the Englishman in question, Christopher Merrett, was more interested in glass than in wine, but he was on the case earlier than the Dom and in December 1662 presented a highly relevant paper to the Royal Society of London.

In *Some Observations concerning the Ordering of Wines* Merrett describes a process of adding quantities of sugar and molasses to make the wine sparkle, the addition stimulating a secondary fermentation in a process the French call the *méthode champenoise*.

His professional interest in glass is significant too, since a conventional wine bottle was at this time simply not strong enough to withstand the pressure of millions of bubbles. Here again it was British ingenuity not French which found the solution, the means of constructing a bottle strong enough to withstand the pressure being devised by Admiral Sir Robert Mansell while the French were still cowering in their *caves* as yet more of their own much feebler vessels continued to explode.

Where is London's **oldest restaurant**?

In October 2009 no fewer than ten dukes – Leinster, Wellington, St Albans, Norfolk, Rutland, Northumberland, Bedford, Somerset, Argyll and Montrose – gathered in the West End in what is thought to have been the largest gathering of their Graces since the Coronation.

The venue for this authentically historic decaducal event was Wilton's in St James's, a restaurant which proudly claims a heritage stretching back more than 250 years, although what is now London's finest fish and seafood restaurant was in 1742 merely a stall selling oysters, shrimps and cockles to shoppers in the Haymarket. The stall may have been humble but business prospered: by 1805 the founder's nephew was able to move into better premises and the new Wilton's Shellfish Mongers and Oyster Rooms in Cockspur Street was soon well on its way to collecting a gaggle of Royal Warrants.

Despite the present restaurant's wonderfully old-fashioned ambience, however, Wilton's as we know it didn't make the move to Jermyn Street until 1984. By that time Thomas Rule's rival enterprise had been in business for almost two centuries, as a fully-fledged restaurant and in precisely the same Covent Garden premises that the red plush banquettes and plethora of antique prints and pictures occupy today.

In 1798 Rule had set out to serve 'porter, pies and oysters' – most of which are still on the menu today, together with some of the best game in season. Admittedly for some the place can feel a bit stagey, and with its memories of famous customers such as Dickens and Wells, Edward VII and Lillie Langtry, that other Edward and Mrs Simpson, it has more than once been likened to a sort of themed-eating experience.

But frankly this is to miss the point entirely, for Rules is real. If the dining rooms at 35 Maiden Lane feel old-fashioned it's because they're very old. Similarly if the menu seems almost comically traditional it's because while there has been the odd addition over the years – these days they even cater for vegetarians – Rules has sensibly stuck to what it knows best: English cooking – meaning pies and puddings, seasonal game, and first-class red meat which is cooked simply and to perfection.

Naturally there have been some changes. Sadly the dress code has been relaxed to the point where there can barely be said to be one. (Presumably to curry favour with tourists, although because of this the excellent staff are now better dressed than nine-tenths of their customers.) Nor are orders any longer stuffed into used shotgun cartridges and dropped down a copper pipe to the kitchens – where until the late 1940s the sound of the brass cartridge cap rattling into a tin tray would have alerted the chef to a new arrival. But the essentials are still in place and, while Rules may no longer quite do it for the dukes, the longest survivor on the London scene will, one hopes, survive another couple of centuries at least.

What was London's most **expensive takeaway**?

Unearthed by Mark Hollingsworth and Stewart Lansley for their fascinating book *Londongrad: From Russia with Cash; The Inside Story of the Oligarchs* – and described by a *Sunday Times* reviewer as epitomising the 'outrageous vulgarity, tastelessness and ruthlessness of people who are wealthy beyond all imagining' – the current title-holder would appear to be the owner of Chelsea Football Club, Roman Abramovich.

According to the book's authors Abramovich once felt the need for some sushi and had an aide order £1,200-worth of it from a favourite Canary Wharf eatery called Ubon. Good sushi is famously expensive, but at the time he conceived his need Abramovich was on a business trip to the Azerbaijani capital Baku. As a result even this impressive total was quickly dwarfed by the expense and logistical challenge of getting a few bits of fresh, raw fish from kitchen to customer.

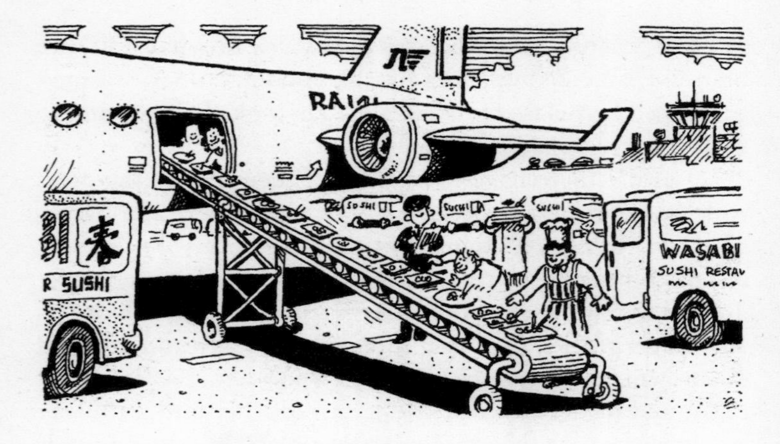

Specifically the takeaway needed to be chauffeur-driven to Luton Airport, from where it was flown – by private jet, obviously – to the former Soviet republic at an estimated cost of £40,000. But doing it this way cannot help but raise a number of pertinent questions. Are there no good restaurants at all in Baku? Is Ubon's food really that good? Does sushi even travel that well? And perhaps most intriguing of all, by the time his order arrived – with Canary Wharf to Baku a good 3,000 miles the takeaway must have taken most of an average working day to complete the distance – was Mr Abramovich climbing the walls with hunger, or had he gone off the sushi idea by then having assuaged his hunger several hours earlier with a more traditional Azerbaijani lunch of *baliq*, *chorek* and *goy*?

Where was London's **first cinema**?

On 18 October 1894 Britain's first commercial film screening took place in a so-called Kinetoscope Parlour at 70 Oxford Street. With Britain's first projector still two years away from going into production (the wonderful sounding Saffron Hill Theatrograph) the proprietors imported twelve machines

from the Continental Commerce Co. of New York. These were used to show such delights as a buxom vaudevillian called *Carmencita* and a demonstration of the blacksmith's art, although the venue was more of a shop than a cinema and today is occupied by an electronics retailer.

The first real cinema was probably the Kineopticon. Situated at the junction of Shaftesbury Avenue and Piccadilly Circus, it opened for business on 21 March 1896 with tickets priced at 6*d*. The first performance included such enticing titles as *The Arrest of a Pickpocket* and *A Visit to the Zoo*, but unfortunately the building was gutted by fire a few weeks later and permanently closed.

Among early filmgoers the royal family was unusually quick to embrace this new-fangled technology, with the Prince of Wales that same year requesting a private viewing in a marquee behind Marlborough House of a film depicting a visit by himself to Cardiff. In November 1896 Queen Victoria similarly watched a film of a number of her relations relaxing at Balmoral, the screening this time taking place in the Red Drawing Room at Windsor Castle.

Visiting an actual cinema was to take the family slightly longer, however, with Queen Alexandra the first royal to do this. In 1907 she went with her friend the Dowager Empress of Russia to a commercial screening in Oslo, but it was to be another six years before an actual sovereign took the plunge with George V going to see *Quo Vadis?* at the Royal Albert Hall. The wait for the first Royal Command Performance to take place in public was to be even longer but finally, on 1 November 1946, George VI and Queen Elizabeth took the young princesses to see David Niven in *A Matter of Life and Death* at the Empire Leicester Square. Such was the spectacle that a crowd began to gather outside some 10 hours before the royals' arrival.

As to the march of technology, the first 'talkie' to be made here – Alfred Hitchcock's *Blackmail* – was premiered in London, at the Marble Arch Regal on 21 June 1929. At the time it was billed as '99 per cent talking' even though the first of two reels contained no dialogue whatsoever. The posters also declared 'See and Hear It – Our Mother Tongue As It Should Be Spoken' in a less than subtle dig at Hollywood's *The Jazz Singer* which had beaten Hitchcock to the screen by a good two years.

Finally for thirty years London was also able to boast that it had the country's largest cinema – the 3,485-seat Art Deco Odeon Hammersmith, formerly the Gaumont Palace and since 1962 a concert venue – as well as its cheapest. A now-defunct cinema in the Whitechapel Road briefly charged just a farthing a head for a group of four children or more purchasing tickets in 1909.

Which is London's **happiest family**?

Certainly a strong claim ought to be made for John Jaques & Son, not just because the company of that name invented the children's card game 'Happy Families', but also because after more than 200 years (and six generations) what is by far the world's oldest sports and games manufacturer is still owned and run by direct descendents of the company's founder. He was one Thomas Jaques, a Wiltshire farmer's son of Huguenot descent, who moving to London set up shop in 1795 in Holborn as a 'manufacturer of Ivory, Hardwoods, Bone and Tunbridge Ware'. Besides the aforementioned card game, succeeding generations of his family have been responsible for so many significant sporting and gaming world-firsts that one wonders how our weekends would be spent were it not for them.

Just a few well documented Jaques innovations include the standardised design of boxwood and ebony chessmen – the knight being based on one of the horses in Britain's Elgin Marbles – also the invention of a number of popular board games including Snakes & Ladders, Tiddlywinks and Ludo. The Jaques family were also responsible for the official formulation of the rules of croquet with the result that (as one commentator put it in 1851) 'nothing but tobacco smoke ever spread more quickly.'

When it came to promoting his new game of Happy Families, John Jaques II decided to commission a series of memorable caricatures from an unknown artist called John Tenniel. Drawing such characters as Mr Bun the Baker and Mr Grits the Grocer, Tenniel later went on to become more widely recognised (and indeed was eventually knighted) after providing the illustrations to Lewis Carroll's *Alice in Wonderland* and *Adventures Through the Looking-Glass*. This John's son, John Jaques III, coincidentally married one of Carroll's great-nieces, as well as proving himself to be just as inventive as his father by introducing yet another new game which caught on every bit as rapidly as croquet.

John III called it 'Gossima' and later 'Ping-Pong' until a new breed of professional sportsmen – a species rarely known for a sense of humour – insisted the name be changed again to the more grown-up table tennis. In turn his son, John IV, promoted a new kind of resin lawn bowl, vastly superior to anything which had gone before, as well as marketing the first ever laminated glassfibre archery bow and the first laminated wooden tennis racket. It was he too who took the company to war, working closely with MI9, the secret intelligence

Department for Escape and Evasion. Together department and company devised some very special games for the three services, containing cleverly concealed maps, banknotes and compasses which are known to have helped literally thousands of PoWs and Commonwealth forces to find their way back home through enemy lines.

8

NATURE

Where's the **best suntan spot** in London?

Camden Square, NW1, has twice returned the highest monthly average temperature – most recently of 35.6 °C in June 1957 – but when it comes to sunshine rather than heat Kew wins hands down. The weather station there recorded a total of 829 hours in June and August 1976, doing so at a time when the average for both months would have been something under 600. (At the other extreme, the records for London in December 1890 show the capital as a whole being denied even a few minutes of weak sunshine for a whole month.)

Those same instruments at the Kew weather station have also logged the chilliest spell on record, however: an uninterrupted run of nine freezing days from 17 to 25 January 1963, a freezing day being a 24-hour period during which the temperature never rises above 0°C. On that occasion it was possible to cross the ice-bound Thames on foot a few miles away at Kingston, although 1963 pales beside the historical record, the two coldest years in the capital having been 1684 and 1740 when enormous 'frost fairs' were held on the Thames.

The temperatures back then were far worse than anything experienced by modern Londoners, and indeed the Thames hasn't frozen downstream of Kingston for nearly 200 years. Even when it last did so, in 1814, it had as much to do with phenomenon known as 'regelation' as it had with air temperature, an unusual feature which arises when a number of large ice floes drifting down to London from colder country districts bond together after becoming wedged in the narrow arches beneath the old London Bridge.

Otherwise London's strangest weather has tended to rely more on weird precipitation than variations in temperature. For example on 1 July 1968 thousands of cars were stained yellow when an estimated 5,000 tons of sand were transported up from the Sahara and washed to the ground in a dramatic thunderstorm. On 2 June 1975 groundsmen at Lord's reported a fall of snow and then two months later – in the middle of an otherwise beautiful summer – more than 6½in of rain fell on Hampstead in less than 2½ hours. Parts of Camden disappeared beneath nearly a foot of hailstorms ¾in in diameter, creating what the *Journal of Meteorology* likened to 'a sea of icy porridge'.

What's the **rarest bird** ever **spotted** in London?

In 1908, digging the 60ft deep foundations of the Royal Automobile Club in Pall Mall, workers uncovered several seventeenth-century cesspits and the fossilised remains of a mammoth. Excavations in Trafalgar Square have likewise thrown up the remains of several prehistoric hippos, bison, bears, elephants and even lions. In recent times, however, the most exotic visitors to London (aside from the odd whale lost in the Thames) have tended to be birds, with an impressive 357 different species being spotted over the capital.

In 2006, for example, the BBC reported that a massive firework display had had to be cancelled when a pair of peregrine falcons set up home close to the site of the Mostly Mozart Festival at the Barbican. The same year scores of twitchers flocked across the river to see a rare American Robin – actually a member of the thrush family, and similar in size to a blackbird – which had been spotted living in Denman Road, close to the station at Peckham Rye. Then in January 2009 a rare Siberian chiffchaff – having flown an estimated 3,000 miles off course – was seen at London Wildlife Trust's East Reservoir Community Garden in Stoke Newington, Hackney.

Unsurprisingly such sightings tend very much to be one-offs, making it hard to decide definitively which individual bird is the rarest. However, of the aforementioned 357 species, examples of the following thirteen have not been seen in London within the last 100 years. None is thought to be extinct but their continued absence is perhaps not quite what one might expect, given that the London Wetland Trust – and work at reservoirs such as the one in Hackney – should in theory make the capital more bird-friendly now than it has been in previous years.

Alpine Accentor	*Prunella collaris*
Baillon's Crake	*Porzana pusilla*
Cream-coloured Courser	*Cursorius cursor*
Golden Eagle	*Aquila chrysaetos*
Great Bustard	*Otis tarda*
Little Crake	*Porzana parva*
Pacific Golden Plover	*Pluvialis fulva*
Parrot Crossbill	*Loxia pytyopsittacus*
Pine Grosbeak	*Pinicola enucleator*
Red-breasted Goose	*Branta ruficollis*
Scops Owl	*Otus scops*
Tengmalm's Owl	*Aegolius funereus*
Two-barred Crossbill	*Loxia leucoptera*

Who were the **Seven Sisters**?

The Seven Sisters which lent their name to an area of Tottenham, North London, are popularly thought to have been a string of elm trees which were planted in a ring to form a sacred grove or possibly a place of execution.

A legend which is popular locally suggests that in the mid-fourteenth century seven elms were planted around a solitary walnut tree by the roadside, this being done at the instigation of seven sisters who were setting off to seek their fortunes in seven different directions. Later a Protestant martyr is said to have been burned on the site, after which the walnut tree failed to fruit or to grow any taller.

True or not the elms were certainly there in the eighteenth century, and in 1833 gave their name to a new turnpike giving improved access from South Tottenham to Westminster. By 1840 the trees were said to be at least 500 years old, it being further suggested that the area in question, by then known as Pages Green, may originally have been called Pagan Green.

Unfortunately within forty years the old trees were gone, although by 1886 another ring had been planted slightly further east – this time by another set of seven sisters, daughters of a local butcher called Hibbert – although this too fell foul of developers or road-builders. It was eventually replaced in 1955 by a third set of seven siblings, this time by the name of Bastin, with each sister planting her own Lombardy poplar.

When was an **elephant** last **hunted** in London?

The Destruction of the Noble Elephant at Mr Cross's Exeter Change, a painting of 1826 ascribed only to the 'English School', illustrates the tragic fate which befell a pet elephant belonging to Mr Edward Cross of the Strand. Correctly called Exeter Exchange, and built on the site of the former home of the earls of that name, the Change in question was an early shopping arcade running off the north side of the Strand opposite to where the Savoy Hotel now stands.

It was eventually demolished as part of an improvement scheme in 1829, but for more than fifty years it was a popular attraction in the city in no small part thanks to the presence of a famous menagerie which Cross and others kept on the upper floors.

From 1773 the first of these showmen had been members of the Pidcock family, circus owners who leased the upper rooms. In competition with the Royal Menagerie at the Tower of London, they filled the rooms with lions, tigers, monkeys and other exotic species which were accommodated in decorated iron cages during the winter months when the circus wasn't touring.

Sometimes, to the horror of horses passing in the Strand, the roaring of the big cats could be heard in the streets below, a sound and spectacle which was hugely popular with Londoners. Later sold to another circus impresario, Stephani Polito, the menagerie was visited by the likes of Byron and Wordsworth as well as Edwin Landseer and the Swiss artist Jacques-Laurent Agasse who came to paint the animals.

In his diary Byron recalled Polito's elephant Chunee (or possibly Chuny) which, 'took and gave me my money again – took off my hat – opened a door – trunked a whip – and behaved so well, that I wished he was my butler.' When his owner died in 1814 the place was taken over by the aforementioned Cross, an employee, who renamed the upper rooms the Royal Grand National Menagerie and employed a doorkeeper whom he dressed in scarlet to look like a Yeoman of the Guard.

Unfortunately over the years the 7-ton Chunee became unmanageable – after appearing at panto at the Theatre Royal Drury Lane, his celebrity had perhaps gone to his head – and his behaviour was becoming increasingly erratic. When the beast ran amok one morning and killed a keeper during his

regular walkabout, Cross was reluctantly forced to bring in soldiers from nearby Somerset House to finish him off. Two of them fired an impressive 152 musket rounds at the unfortunate beast before one of the other keepers ordered the injured animal to kneel so he could finish him off with blade attached to a long pole.

While hundreds had no problem with this and paid a shilling to see his carcass being butchered, many others objected to the elephant's violent death (and to recipes for elephant stew being circulated by pamphleteers) and Exeter Change rapidly declined in popularity.

With the other animals being dispersed to the new London Zoological Gardens in Regent's Park, Chunee's 876lb skeleton was sold for £100 and exhibited at the Egyptian Hall in Piccadilly. The bullet holes were clearly visible, but even then poor old Chunee had not quite suffered his last: one final indignity was visited upon him when his remains – by now on display at the Royal College of Surgeons – received a direct hit from a Luftwaffe bomb in 1941 and were destroyed.

Where is the **oldest tree** in London?

In April 2008 a quite ordinary plane tree in Mayfair's Berkeley Square was valued at £750,000 in accordance with a bizarre local authority scheme requiring insurers to assess the value of a tree – depending on its size, health, history and how many people lived nearby – before deciding to chop it down. One of thirty-one trees in the square described as 'valuable', the plane in question thus became London's most expensive tree.

It did so despite being just 200 years old; that is, a mere sapling compared to the capital's oldest which is up the road in Regent's Park. Actually the tree in question is so old it's just a stump, a fossilised stump at that, being the last surviving remnant of the gardens of the former Royal Botanic Society which was housed here from 1839 to 1932. It was brought to

London from the Jurassic coast of Dorset, a place where this type of conifer once thrived in the hot and arid conditions then prevailing before the coastline was inundated by hypersaline seawater and the tree preserved as quartz.

But if that one doesn't count on the grounds that it's dead, then London's oldest tree is thought to be a gnarly old yew growing in the churchyard of St Andrew's, Totteridge Lane in Barnet. The eighteenth-century church itself was built on the site of a chapel with origins dating back to 1250. But the tree was clearly ancient even then, with experts from the Conservation Foundation and the wonderfully self-explanatory Ancient Yew Group confidently asserting that it could now be as much as 2,000 years old.

Measuring some 25ft all the way round, but like many yews hollowed-out with age making it difficult to date precisely by counting the rings, the tree was first mentioned by the Revd Sir John Cullum Bt of Bury St Edmunds, in 1677. A successful City draper and keen amateur botanist, Sir John put its girth at 26ft, and in 1722 the tree was on record as having provided shelter for an abandoned baby who was raised by the parish after being christened Henry Totteridge. It is also thought to have been used as a meeting point for hundreds of years before this, and even as the setting for so-called 'hundred courts' in which local disputes would have been settled.

Meanwhile, on a much smaller scale, the authorities at Kew Gardens announced in July 2009 that they were re-potting 'the oldest pot plant in the world'. The plant in question is a cycad weighing one tonne and brought to Kew by its first plant-hunter, Francis Mason, in the early 1770s. Mason located the plant in South Africa's Eastern Cape and recognising it as an ancient species realised that it could provide valuable clues about the nature of early plants. In theory it could outlive a man by as much as 500 years, meaning that it is even now barely approaching middle age.

9

CRIME

What is London's most **shoplifted book**?

You'd think it would be *Steal This Book*, a volume published in 1971 by the 'yippie' radical and social activist Abbie Hoffman which offered readers advice on shoplifting, setting up a pirate radio station, living in communes and a variety of other crimes which the controversialist author argued constituted valid form of public protest. But sadly not: while you can still buy a brand new copy on Amazon for £36, most booksellers at the time simply refused to stock it, a few perhaps reluctant to join the revolution but most, one suspects, simply concerned that they would lose money by doing so.

Aside from this one, common sense suggests the most shoplifted book would also have to be the biggest-selling – in which case it would have to be the Bible, although stealing a copy of the Bible would be bit bizarre, to say the least. In fact cult fiction and fantasy fiction seem to be especially popular among light-fingered readers, something which puts Terry Pratchett's stuff somewhere near the top in the UK.

In other genres Irvine Welsh probably helped his own ranking by including on the cover of *Trainspotting* an urgent (and slightly Hoffmanesque) instruction for readers to beg, steal or borrow the book. Meanwhile in the Antipodes Australia's *Bookseller and Publisher* magazine claims that the three most consistent performers for more than fifteen years have been *South East Asia on a Shoestring*, *Junkie* by William Burroughs and Jack Kerouac's *On The Road*. The first of these suggests a practical rather than philosophical leaning, and indeed the same would appear to be true here in London where the *London A–Z* – eminently useful, definitive and handily pocket-sized – has traditionally been the most shoplifted book in the capital.

Rising at dawn in the mid-1930s, and tramping more than 3,000 miles down 23,000 streets in a year, the redoubtable Phyllis Pearsall (1906–96) compiled the first one, self-published the finished volume when no-one else would touch it, and delivered her first ink-fresh copies to W.H. Smith in a wheelbarrow. Her inspiration was said to have been a wasted winter evening spent walking around Belgravia in the rain, clutching a damp, out-of-date Ordnance Survey map and failing to find the correct address for a party to which she had been invited.

Once started, the research had all to be done on foot, and as she said at the time she would walk 'down one street, find three more and have no idea where I was.' Back then the Roedean- and Sorbonne-educated Mrs Pearsall's most sincere hope was that she'd make enough money from the project to pay for her real passion which was painting; in fact it turned out the other way round with the occasional sale of one of her paintings being used to underwrite the cost of her map-making excursions. Eventually she had enough to pay for a print run of 10,000 – covering everywhere from Aaron Hill to Zoffany Street, hence the memorable name – and when she died just short of her 90th birthday she was still working at the Geographer's A–Z Map Company which has so far produced nearly 360 different titles based on her one brilliant original.

How long does it take to **boil a criminal**?

A full two hours apparently, assuming one starts with a cauldron of cold water which seems to have been the preferred recipe for such occasions at Smithfield in the sixteenth century.

At that time, specifically from 1531 until 1547, an Act was in force permitting boiling as a form of capital punishment, a cook called Richard Rose or Roose being the first to find himself on the receiving end of such a cruel and unusual punishment after he was convicted of adding poison to food and killing a number of individuals in the process.

The next to go was a servant girl up in King's Lynn who had murdered her mistress, but even in London during the peak years boiling alive was used only very rarely. This didn't prevent the exceptional gruesomeness of the process capturing the general imagination, however, and for a long while the term 'William Boilman' joined the list of nicknames which attached themselves to various public executioners.

The public's gory fascination with such things is of course well known, and not as hard to comprehend as the more liberal-minded occasionally affect to believe. What is surprising, however, is that the death penalty has been used most often in more recent times, with many of the most barbaric and horrific refinements being devised relatively late on.

A thousand years ago, before the Conquest, an offender was more likely to be thrown to his death off a cliff than to fall prey to some fiendish contraption. Likewise the early Normans were sparing in their use of the ultimate sanction, with both Williams I and II employing it only against traitors.

It wasn't until the twelfth century and the reign of Henry I that its use was extended to convicted murderers, and not until much later – the Waltham Black Act of 1723, also known as the 'Bloody Code' – that capital punishment began to be prescribed for all sorts of minor crimes. By late 1815 more than 200 offences were listed in the Code, including poaching a rabbit, stealing a turnip, consorting with gypsies, impersonating a Chelsea Pensioner, even being out after dark with a sooty face.

For such offences hanging was generally the preferred means of despatch, being both easier to arrange and decidedly tidier than your average beheading. Nor was age or immaturity any defence and in the nineteenth century one 13-year-old boy was hanged for stealing a spoon together with a 9-year-old arsonist and a 7-year-old girl for a crime so petty that 200 years later the records don't even show what it was.

Occasionally for more serious offences (although often not that serious, actually) the authorities continued to sanction other means. Burning at the stake, for example, was sometimes employed against common criminals, in particular women convicted of coining – counterfeiting or clipping the edges of gold and silver coins – or of 'petty treason', i.e. murdering their husbands.

Here, at least, attempts were frequently made to alleviate the suffering, either by hanging bags of gunpowder around the victim's neck to ensure a speedier despatch or more commonly by strangling them before the fire had been lit. Certainly the last person to go this way – convicted coiner Christine Murphy, on 18 March 1789 – was dead before the flames took hold, the stool on which she had been standing outside Newgate Gaol having been kicked away before the faggots had been put in place around her feet.

What's so **posh** about getting the **chop**?

Even in death noblemen have traditionally enjoyed a number of privileges, perhaps the best-known being the right to be hanged with a silk cord instead of hemp rope – a rather questionable entitlement popularly but erroneously said to have been claimed by the servant-murdering Earl Ferrers in 1760.

From the fifteenth century aristocrats and other establishment figures could also opt to undergo a form of torture known as *peine forte et dure,* (from the French for 'hard and forceful punishment'). This involved being pressed to death beneath a wooden board loaded with weights, a slow and hideously painful process the only advantage of which was to escape forfeiture by the Crown of one's property which would otherwise follow a guilty plea or conviction.

In this way members of the landed classes were able to ensure that their heirs could inherit their estates, a loophole which remained in place until 1772. Thereafter the law was changed so that anyone refusing to plead was automatically considered to have made a guilty plea – unlike today when anyone accused of a crime who chooses to stand mute is considered by the court to have entered a plea of not guilty.

Judicial beheading, public or otherwise, was for a long time also reserved for aristocrats. Being considered a privilege of rank, it was thought to be an honourable death akin to dying in battle whereas being hanged – with or without the additional indignities of being drawn and quartered – was decidedly dishonourable. Beheading was generally a quicker way to go too, the death being instantaneous (unlike hanging) – at least if the job was done correctly and with a suitably sharp blade.

That said, Mary, Queen of Scots and the Earl of Essex each required three strikes, and in 1541 it took a total of eleven blows to finally silence the 67-year-old Catholic martyr, Margaret Pole, Countess of Salisbury. Similarly in 1685 when the infamous Jack Ketch – almost certainly drunk at the time – was charged with decapitating the Duke of Monmouth on Tower Hill he took five swings with his axe before eventually pulling out a pocket knife to finish the grisly task.

Elsewhere in the country, especially up north, a number of attempts were made to avoid this kind of spectacle, typically by devising mechanical machines such as the 'Scottish Maiden' and the 'Halifax Gibbet'. These two preceded by some years the famous French decapitator named after Dr Joseph-Ignace Guillotin – which, incidentally, was still in use in France as recently as 1977 – but neither ever quite caught on down south. Londoners preferred to stick with the axe, and on 1 May 1820 five of the Cato Street conspirators enjoyed the highly dubious distinction of being the very last to be publicly beheaded in London after being found guilty of plotting to topple the government by murdering Lord Liverpool and his ministers.

What was the **stupidest** thing ever **left on a train**?

Franz Muller's hat, no question. In 1919 Lt-Col. Thomas Edward Lawrence CB, DSO mislaid his briefcase while changing trains at Reading, a briefcase which unfortunately for its owner contained a 250,000-word manuscript detailing his wartime exploits. For Lawrence of Arabia, as he is now better known as, it was a considerable loss which required him to redraft from memory an even longer version which eventually saw the light of day as *The Seven Pillars of Wisdom*. He himself thought the experience 'hopelessly bad' although by any reckoning his loss was nothing compared to that of Herr Muller's half a century earlier.

On 9 July 1864, travelling on a train operated by the North London Railway between Fenchurch Street and Hackney Wick, the jobbing tailor found himself sharing a compartment with a bank official called Thomas Briggs. After robbing him of his gold watch and chain (and a pair of spectacles) he heaved the banker's badly beaten body through the carriage window and assuming him to be dead alighted from the train at the next station.

The unfortunate Briggs did indeed die of his injuries, but in a pub adjacent to the railway where he had been taken after the driver of another train spotted his body lying by the tracks. Meanwhile two other City workers boarding the first train at Hackney Wick discovered a pool of blood in the compartment and a distinctive black beaver hat belonging to Muller who had carelessly wandered off wearing his victim's headgear rather than his own.

The first ever murder on Britain's new-fangled railway not unnaturally caused a huge furore, the murderer fleeing to New York when he heard that a £300 reward was being offered for his capture. On his arrival he was promptly arrested by two Scotland Yard detectives who had travelled to the new world on a faster ship. He was also found to be wearing the very hat stolen from his victim, although during the voyage he had used his tailoring skills to modify it by lowering the crown. Charged with murder and returned to London, he stood trial at Newgate, was found guilty and was sentenced to hang on 14 November 1864.

Even with tickets to view the execution from the surrounding buildings going for up to £10 a seat (at a time when a farmhand or general labourer might do well to earn a pound a week) the crowd which assembled to see Muller's end was vast. It was also unruly and becoming ugly, with the ensuing disorder contributing to the decision just four years later to call a halt to public executions. The legacy of Muller's crime went further than that, however, with railway companies taking steps to install communication cords in their carriages (on the grounds that if Briggs had been able to contact the guard he might not have been killed), and the fashion for a new style of hat called the 'Muller Cut-Down' continuing until well into the twentieth century.

Where's the most **crime-ridden** place in **London**?

Thamesmead, according to identity fraud-prevention experts The 3rd Man Group. In September 2009 the company released a set of figures showing that when it comes to credit card fraud the police nickname given to this south-east London enclave – Little Lagos – is well-earned, with a staggering £1 in every three spent in the area almost certainly fraudulent.

Across Britain as a whole an estimated £1,000 a minute is scammed using various different kinds of identity fraud, but as in so many fields London leads the way with organised gangs efficiently fleecing punters and businesses of hundreds of millions annually. Frequently this is done by stealing mail from communal letterboxes in blocks of flats, and applying for new cards in their victims' names. This simple but effective method in 2008 led to high-rise Thamesmead being described as the fraud capital of Britain, an assessment which the following year was extended to include the whole of Europe.

Speaking to the BBC in 2009 one fraud expert said he knew of a street in the district where every single house was implicated in such crimes, although he refused to name the street on the grounds that some householders would be victims rather than perpetrators and wouldn't even know about it unless they had applied for a legitimate loan or card themselves. Local police, too, recognise the area's pre-eminence in this sort of crime, one officer telling journalists that Thamesmead is 'rife with credit card fraud. The gangs ship their own people here, putting them up in houses to create a network trading in card details and fraudulently buying expensive goods.'

Needless to say many near-identical systems operate elsewhere in the capital too: in High Barnet a sixth of all online transactions are known to be fraudulent, while the figure for East Finsbury is closer to £1 in five. But perhaps no-one should be surprised that it's so much worse in dingy Thamesmead. The place may have started out as some kind of 1960s dream vision but – stark, self-contained and strangely isolated – these days if it is known at all it is as the setting for the film *A Clockwork Orange,* Stanley Kubrick's bleakly violent and horribly dystopic vision of the near future.

London's Top 10 Postcodes for Financial Fraud:

(% of credit card transactions shown to be fraudulent)

DA17	East Thamesmead and Erith Marshes	34.0%
SE28	Thamesmead	26.3%
SE2	South Thamesmead and Crossness	24.4%
EC1V	East Finsbury	20.0%
EN5	High Barnet	16.3%
EC1R	Finsbury & Clerkenwell	16.3%
RM19	Purfleet	16.3%
RM10	Dagenham	16.2%
SE18	Woolwich	15.7%
DA8	Erith	15.3%

Who was **Gordon** and why was he **rioting**?

A passionate eighteenth-century Protestant right up until the moment he converted to Judaism, and the son of a duke who nevertheless led a populist revolt, Lord George Gordon (1751–93) was also the man through whose exertions half of London was trashed. Yet when he was finally gaoled it wasn't for visiting wholesale destruction upon the capital, but merely for libelling a foreign queen.

These days if anyone remembers Gordon at all it is for the eponymous riots of June 1780. An orgy of violence which over several days saw as many as 20,000 troops on the streets of the capital, the Gordon Riots led to the deaths of more than 800 Londoners with 450 others being arrested, a third of them indicted, and more than two dozen executed. Somehow Gordon himself evaded censure more or less completely after being acquitted of a most serious charge of high treason.

As a Member of Parliament and leader of the Protestant Association, Lord George had organised a meeting at the

Coachmakers' Hall in Noble Street and encouraged a 50,000-strong march from Southwark to Westminster to protest against plans to repeal Britain's numerous anti-Catholic laws. In this he was in one sense largely successful: under the terms of the more than 300-year-old Act of Settlement a Catholic and indeed anyone married to a Catholic is still barred from the throne. Nevertheless, in June 1780, his position looked less secure as he rapidly lost control of a crowd which had been whipped up into a positive frenzy of anti-Catholic feeling by a variety of concerns about Rome-inspired conspiracies, Papal plots and the usual, largely groundless superstition.

Very soon his lordship's supporters were running amok, burning and looting Catholic houses (or houses presumed to be Catholic), attacking Irishmen in the street, plundering the private chapels of the Sardinian and Bavarian ambassadors, and torching two more on the edge of the City.

Eventually, inevitably, members of the mob turned against each other and directed their anger towards a number of public buildings. Razing five prisons to the ground – Newgate, Clerkenwell, the Fleet, King's Bench and the Borough Clink – they attacked Downing Street and then the Bank of England where the clerks fought a magnificent defensive action by firing bullets manufactured by melting-down their ink wells. George III summoned his Dragoons onto the streets to fire on a mob which was by now so drunk – Langdale's Distillery in Holborn had been an early casualty – that many of the hundreds of fatalities were caused not by gunfire but by intoxicated rioters falling into the flames of burning buildings to emerge like human torches.

With order finally restored, their hapless leader was locked in the Tower for nearly eight months, charged with high treason and then set free on the grounds that he had merely lost control of the crowd rather than egging them on.

Steps were taken to ensure nothing similar happened again, however – an armed Bank Guard or piquet marched down Threadneedle Street every night, and continued to stand guard there until the early 1970s – and eventually Lord George got his just desserts when a libel against Marie-Antoinette took him to the rebuilt Newgate where in time he died. Reportedly a happy prisoner who kept himself busy, the duke's son played the bagpipes to amuse himself and his fellow inmates, and frequently entertained six or eight guests to dinner.

Who was the **first** London **copper** to be **killed** on duty?

Kicked hard in the head while trying to break up a drunken brawl in Somers Town near King's Cross on 28 June 1830, PC Joseph Grantham became the first officer to die on duty just a year after the Met's foundation.

Prior to 1829 the only police in London were those on the river, magistrates Patrick Colquhoun and John Harriot having founded what was then the Marine Police Force in 1798, the world's first and oldest constabulary. Their force was established specifically to combat theft from shipping, with companies operating in the Pool of London admitting to losing fully half their cargo before it had even left the docks and one in every three dockers assumed to be a thief or a receiver.

With an estimated 100,000 Londoners also thought to be criminals at this time, something similar was clearly needed on the streets as well. Within a year of its foundation Sir Robert Peel's new Metropolitan Police Force had recruited an impressive 3,000 men to the task, dressed in dark blue swallow-tail coats (similar to a senior servant, in order to demonstrate the civilian nature of their role) and top hats as a sign of their respectability and authority.

The hat also made the officer look taller, and helped people to recognise a copper in a crowd, while its internal cane reinforcement meant the wearer could safely stand on it to peer over walls.

In those days discipline was as strict as the wages were low, a new constable earning a guinea a week in exchange for which he had to report for duty for seven shifts a week, walk an average of 20 miles each and every shift regardless of the weather, and to refrain from sitting down on the job or being seen to lean against anything while out and about on duty.

He was also only lightly armed, sporting no more than a short copper-bound truncheon – hence his nickname – and a rattle to summon help. The latter was subsequently upgraded to a whistle, and eventually the hat disappeared being too easily knocked off by missiles thrown by a largely unappreciative public. How unappreciative? Well let's just say that a jury returned a verdict of justifiable homicide in the case of PC Grantham, on the grounds that he had effectively caused his own death by 'over exertion in the discharge of his duty'.

What's **London's** most **unlikely** murder **weapon**?

Colonel Mustard on the Waterloo and City Line with an Oyster card? Well only if you've not got an umbrella handy, since this has been the weapon of choice in at least two of London's most notorious murders. The first was the killing of a petty thief called 'Bulldog' Wallis, stabbed in the eye with an umbrella in the aptly named Blind Beggar on Whitechapel Road.

The most famous brolly murder, however, was definitely that of Georgi Markov, a prize-winning Bulgarian author and broadcaster who felt a slight sting in his leg while waiting for a bus on Waterloo Bridge in September 1978. Assuming he'd simply been accidentally jostled by the rush-hour crowds – a thick-set man had even apologised for bumping into him – the BBC World Service journalist died three days later, whereupon it was discovered that he had been stabbed in the thigh.

A high-profile exile from Communism, Markov had received several death threats before and, having been warned in an anonymous telephone call that he would eventually be poisoned, he had made a point of eating only at home or in the company of friends.

His death, when it came, was a piece of spy theatre worthy of Bond at his best: the murder weapon an umbrella specially modified by the Soviet KGB; the ammunition a single pinhead-sized platinum/iridium pellet containing the toxin ricin; and the identity of Markov's killer destined to remain a secret until well into the next century. Indeed even when the truth about the killer finally did leak out (nearly thirty years later), it was as tangled as any movie plot and contained plenty of wriggle-room if anyone fancied planning a sequel.

After the fall of the Berlin Wall and the subsequent upheavals, a search of Bulgaria's secret service headquarters revealed a pile of similarly customised umbrellas, although it turned out that the Markov job itself had been subcontracted out to a Danish hitman of Italian extraction.

Hiding behind the code-name 'Agent Piccadilly', one Francesco Giullino had spent much of the 1970s travelling round Europe disguised as an art dealer and was almost certainly responsible for a similar attack on a second Bulgarian broadcaster, Vladimir Kostov. Kostov had survived, protected by a thick woollen cardigan, but in 1993 his likely assailant disappeared and while those close to the case insisted on telling a *Times* reporter that 'nothing bad has happened to him' the Italo-Scandinavian hitman has never been seen again.

Who was **Jack** the **Ripper**?

Active for just four months in late 1888, and with a relatively modest tally of just five victims, no other serial killer has exercised quite such a hold on the British imagination or garnered quite so many theories as to who was responsible and how, precisely, he, she or they got away with it.

An internet search on the phrase 'Jack the Ripper' throws up well over 2,000,000 pages, many of them leading to dedicated websites whose authors are still trying to pin a real name on him. Similarly, on Amazon the number of Jack videos and Jack DVDs is dwarfed only by the avalanche of books offering everything from fictionalised accounts of the murders themselves to hugely detailed theories as to who might have done it and why. Elsewhere in the digital universe, Ripper fans have a choice of themed video and computer games; they can buy a 1963 single about the murders by 'Screaming' Lord Sutch (at the time it was swiftly banned by the BBC), and as late as 1934 the celebrated wigmaker Willy Clarkson of Wardour Street was still claiming to have inadvertently provided a disguise for the evil Jack.

Naturally a major part of the appeal is that very little is certain about the Ripper beyond the fact that nobody knows his identity. We know the names of his victims – Mary Ann Nichols, Annie Chapman, Elizabeth Stride, Catherine Eddowes and Mary Jane Kelly – and their uniformly gory ends have clearly helped to fan the flames, as have rumours of a Masonic conspiracy or two, and the obvious cinematic possibilities offered by the smoggy, late-Victorian East End. All told, more than 100 suspects have been put in the frame at one time or another, of which the most interesting – which is not at all to say the most plausible – are those shown below.

The Public School Boy: Montague John Druitt (1857–88). Educated at Winchester and New College, Oxford, Druitt was a barrister of the Inner Temple until his stone-weighted corpse was found bumping around in the Thames near Chiswick. This was shortly after the fifth and final murder, and led the police to name him as a possible suspect.

The Shifty Foreigner: Seweryn Antonowicz Klosowski (1865–1903). A Pole who on the one hand murdered three barmaids but on the other chose to do it with poison. Unfortunately for suspect hunters, most serial killers tend to pick a method which works for them and stick with it, meaning it is highly unlikely that Klosowski would suddenly switch to ritually disembowelling his victims.

The Royal Connection: Sir William Withey Gull Bt (1816–90). Physician-in-Ordinary to HM Queen Victoria and frequently named in connection with a variety of royal and/or Masonic conspiracies connected with the murders. In recent years the hapless baronet has popped up in books, films and even a graphic novel.

The Wife-Murderer: William Bury (1859–89). A convicted wife-murderer and one who inflicted strange wounds on the corpse of his spouse, the sometime prostitute Ellen Eliot, leading to suggestions that he might be the man. However, when he confessed to killing his wife – for which he was hanged at Dundee – he made no mention of any similar activities down in London.

The Hanged Man: Thomas Neill Cream (1850–92). A doctor specialising in illegal abortions and found guilty of a number of murders here and in the US, Cream is occasionally reported to have uttered the words 'I am Jack the . . .' as the trapdoor opened on the gallows. However, official witnesses at his execution make no claims to have heard any such thing.

The Madman: Thomas Hayne Cutbush (1864–1903). A certified lunatic, Cutbush was sent to Broadmoor after stabbing one woman and attempting to wound another. He was, even so, never officially a suspect for any of the Whitechapel murders although many amateur Ripper-watchers have pointed the finger.

The Celebrity: Charles Lutwidge Dodgson (1832–98). As Lewis Carroll, the author of *Alice in Wonderland* and *Adventures Through the Looking-Glass* has also been mentioned in connection with the murders. The evidence for this is that certain passages of his books are said to contain secret, anagrammatic confessions to the crimes – but most serious scholars know that such an idea is simply too good to be true.

The Society Painter: Walter Richard Sickert (1860–1942). The German-born English artist was another famous name which appealed to the conspiracy theorists, an idea which has proved irresistible to several novelists although no evidence of his involvement has ever come to light. More likely is that the cosmopolitan Sickert was in France at the time the murders actually took place.

The Prince: HRH Albert Victor Christian Edward (1864–92). A bit of a royal wrong 'un and known to all as Eddy, the Duke of Clarence and Avondale – George V's older brother – wasn't mentioned as a suspect until well into the 1960s. Thereafter the idea took hold that he had been motivated to commit the murders after going mad as a consequence of contracting syphilis – or possibly to conceal an illegal marriage he'd contracted with a Catholic commoner with whom he had produced an heir. Almost certainly wrong on every count – not just because he had some very robust alibis – the dying flames of suspicion have nevertheless been kept alive by the credulous.

10

LONDON AT WAR

When was the **first air-raid** on London?

The classic image is almost always of the Blitz: St Paul's wreathed in smoke and noise and chaos, or one of Henry Moore's celebrated studies of the huddled masses sheltering in the Tube. But the reality is that the first bombs rained down on the capital a quarter of a century earlier, *The Times* warning its readers in May 1915 that, 'Germany is talking about the coming invasion of London by a fleet of Zeppelins, possibly accompanied by other forms of aircraft'.

The same report described a new and highly destructive type of *nebelbomben* or fog-bomb but in the event the first attack took place a couple of weeks later, the German army Zeppelin *LZ38* making good the Kaiser's hope that 'the air war against England be carried out with the greatest energy' but doing so using conventional explosives.

Looming over London on 31 May, the dirigible quickly scored a direct hit on a crowded house at 16 Alkham Road, Stoke Newington, before going on to bomb properties nearby. A total of seven lives were lost, with a further thirty-five injured.

The choice of target would have been entirely incidental, the aircrew's willingness to make good their leader's wish being frustrated by both the primitive nature of early air-navigation systems and fairly rudimentary bomb-aiming equipment.

Civilian casualties were therefore initially fairly low (at least compared to battlefield levels) but the shock value of the new technology was very considerable. With witnesses reporting terrifying mechanical sounds in the air and the rush of a wholly unnatural wind, the youngest victim was 3-year-old Elsie Leggatt, cremated where she lay after crawling under her bed to hide.

Aware of the level of public concern, and with better organised and more sustained raids being launched in 1917, the authorities let it be known that stations on the Underground would from now on be available to shelter anyone caught out and about when one of these new air raids began. Londoners didn't need to be told twice, and before long the *Railway Gazette* was grumbling that station platforms 'in all parts of London were crowded with men, women and children [and] a large number of pet dogs which accompanied their owners into safety.' At the same time the Circle Line experienced a huge boom (as it were) with hundreds making seemingly endless journeys around the loop as the bombs continued falling overhead.

On occasion the crowding proved problematic, however, with the *Gazette* recording a panic at Liverpool Street among 'people of the poorer classes, mostly aliens, women and children' when one female was trampled to death. The peak came one night in February 1918 when an estimated 300,000 took to the Tube during a raid – a far higher total than at any time during more destructive Blitz of the 1940s.

. . . And the **last**?

On 10 July 2005. Marking 60 years since the end of the Second World War – and choosing to do so on the midway point between VE Day and VJ Day – several hundred thousand people crowded into the Mall, the volume of their chatter suddenly dropping away as ears strained to hear the distinctive beat of six powerful Rolls-Royce V12 Merlin engines powering towards Buckingham Palace from the far side of Trafalgar Square.

The engines in question belonged to the Supermarine Spitfire, Hawker Hurricane and ultra-rare Avro Lancaster of the Royal Air Force Battle of Britain Memorial Flight, the historic, heroic trio charged with making an especially low pass on this very special day. The flypast was to be particularly unusual in that the four-engined Lancaster *P474*, Britain's last airworthy example of this celebrated heavy bomber, was to pass over with its bomb doors open.

The reason was that Marshal of the Royal Air Force Sir Michael Beetham and his crew were to shower those watching below with thousands upon thousands of red poppies. Indeed just moments after the aircraft appeared over Admiralty Arch, there were literally a million of them, slowly drifting in a vivid blood-red stain across the bright blue sky, a moving gesture of thanks for what the modern RAF described as 'the immense contribution played by the wartime generation to our freedom today.'

A simple, symbolic exercise which took only seconds to execute, this unique poppy-drop had nevertheless taken a good deal of planning and nearly three weeks to prepare for.

Apparently it takes an experienced crew of three a full working week, for example, just to remove the bomb cradles from the bay. Thereafter, and without damaging or altering the fabric of this irreplaceable aircraft, the same crew had to fit a shield to protect the aircraft's complex and delicate mechanical systems from being clogged by any stray blooms.

Once this was done the process of loading the poppies – all purchased and paid for from the Royal British Legion – took another three days, a layer of red paper and plastic some 3ft deep having to be ladled into the aircraft by hand through a tiny hatch inside at the rear of the bomb aimer's compartment. It was also considered a sensible precaution to temporarily disable the normal cockpit control for the bomb doors, if only to prevent the crew from accidentally jettisoning their load prematurely on their way into London.

Once the aircraft had been through its usual pre-flight checks, *P474* was finally ready for the off. Well, nearly anyway. With the aircraft making its way to London from the former RAF base at Duxford in Cambridgeshire (where the day before it had taken part in the Imperial War Museum's fabulous Flying Legends Air Show) careful calculations and wind measurements had first to be made in order to know precisely when and where to press the red button. Only then could the strange cargo take to the air and be released into the airflow over central St James's. Left to stream out some 1,500 yards behind the Lancaster, the poppies floated gently but precisely down on to the Mall below. Mission accomplished, and so movingly.

Why did so many **evacuees return** to **London** once the **bombing started?**

As early as 1934, less than a year after Hitler had come to power, secret plans were already well advanced to move children and vulnerable adults out of London in the event of another war with Germany. Some attempts were made to protect the civilian population of the capital – for example, by excavating hundreds of yards of deep trenches and armoured bunkers beneath Lincoln's Inn Fields – but by the 1938 Munich Crisis it was obvious that the huge numbers required more drastic action.

The preferred alternative was to move more of them out, and it is now estimated that as many as 3,500,000 people left the most vulnerable urban areas within a week of war being declared on 3 September 1939. Some, around 5,000, left for North America, but the vast majority were removed to the countryside.

Detailed plans had long been in place to relocate key government departments, so that parts of the BBC were dispersed to Bristol and Worcestershire, the Bank of England went to Overton in Hampshire, and pictures from the National Gallery were safely stacked in racks deep underground in

a disused Welsh slate mine. It was natural that the staff of these institutions would follow, as well as many hundreds of thousands of children once their parents had agreed to let them go.

As a logistical exercise it was brilliantly organised, with more than three-quarters of a million youngsters moved out of the capital in a mere three days. The trip was to come as the profoundest shock to many of them, however. Not just because they were to be separated from their homes and families for the first time, but also because many of the children of the working classes had literally never left the streets in which they were born.

The novelty made the move a very real voyage of discovery – one small boy wrote back, 'they call this spring, Mum, and they have one down here every year' – but for many it was traumatic, with Jewish refugees as young as five being sent packing in the middle of the night by householders in Cornwall on the grounds that they weren't about to welcome any 'bloody Germans' into their homes.

Others strongly objected to the idea of opening their rose-bowered front doors to many English children too, especially those they viewed as wild and unsanitary Cockney tykes. The story of the mother telling her weak-bladdered child, 'don't do it on the nice lady's chair but up against the wall like we do at home,' may be apocryphal. But a member of Churchill's government (the future Lord Chandos, who agreed to take ten evacuees and got thirty) recorded in his memoirs that he had no idea children raised in this country could be so ignorant of the rules of hygiene as to 'regard the floors and carpets as suitable places upon which to relieve themselves.'

Perhaps unsurprisingly the shock on both sides, and the less than warm reception, led more than 300,000 Londoners to return to the city in the early months of the war, with many city children simply refusing to eat the wholesome, natural food which grew all around them and instead, in the words of one report, 'clamouring for fish and chips, biscuits and sweets.'

Many of the young and expectant mothers who accompanied them felt much the same way too, 'missing the neighbours, the shops, the gossipy streets' and deciding to return home as soon as they could.

Even so, once the bombers started making regular raids they had to take some steps towards self-preservation, especially when the V1 and V2 rockets began making their presence felt. But many Londoners preferred 'trekking' to full-time country life – leaving the city each night to find sanctuary, as many thousands did by camping in Epping Forest – or indeed the relative discomfort of a bunkbeds and bedbugs on the Underground to moving out lock, stock and barrel. In times of trouble, after all, familiarity can be a highly effective safety blanket, and perhaps that's why more than 60 per cent of Londoners continued to sleep in their own beds right through until 1945.

How **bad** was the **Blitz**?

With an estimated 20,000 killed and 180,000 injured, the effect on morale was far more serious than the numbers alone would suggest, particularly when these are viewed against the background of a war which claimed a total of more than 50 million lives worldwide.

The damage to the fabric of the capital was certainly very substantial, however. Not just in the docks where the Germans' clear intention was to fatally disrupt commercial life in London, but across the entire city. In all, around 1.4 million homes – a full third of the capital's entire housing stock – were badly damaged or destroyed, with electricity, gas and water supplies regularly cut off.

Besides people's homes a huge number of important or historic public buildings took a hit too, some of the better known ones being shown below:

All Hallows-by-the-Tower
All Hallows-on-the-Wall
All Saints Notting Hill
Arsenal Stadium
Bakers Row, EC1
Balham Tube station
Bank Tube station
Big Ben
Bounds Green station
British Museum
Buckingham Palace
Café de Paris
Central Telegraph Office
Chelsea Old Church
Christ Church, Newgate
Dutch Church
Euston station
Free Trade Hall
The Great Synagogue
Guildhall
Holland House
Houses of Parliament
Lambeth Palace
Lambeth Walk
London Library
Marble Arch Tube station
National Portrait Gallery
Old Bailey
Palace Theatre
Paternoster Row
Shell Mex House
St Joseph's School
St Alban, Wood Street
St Alfege's Church, Greenwich
St Andrew-by-the-Wardrobe
St Andrew Holborn
St Ann's Church
St Augustine Watling Street
St Bartholomew the Less
St Botolph's Aldersgate
St Clement Danes
St Dunstan-in-the-East
St George-in-the-East
St James Garlickhythe
St James's Palace
St Lawrence Jewry
St Mary Abchurch
St Mary Aldermanbury
St Mary-le-Bow
St Nicholas Cole Abbey
St Olave Hart Street
St Paul's Cathedral
St Vedast-alias-Foster
Temple Church
Westminster Abbey
Westminster Hall

Where is the world's **largest collection** of **Victoria Crosses**?

With more than sixty holders of the Victoria Cross buried in London cemeteries, and the medals themselves still cast from captured gunmetal only by the London jeweller Hancocks & Co. of Burlington Arcade, it is appropriate that from the autumn of 2010 a specially built gallery in London's Imperial War Museum will house in excess of 200 VCs, more than any other institution in the world.

The core of the collection, numbering 150 at the time of writing and representing substantially in excess of a tenth of all the Victoria Crosses ever gazetted, has taken nearly a quarter of a century to assemble. The collector, Lord Ashcroft of Chichester, acquired his first in 1986 by way of honouring a promise he made as a schoolboy that if his circumstances ever permitted it he would one day buy and own a VC.

At that time it was expected that the purchase of the medal won and worn by Seaman James Magennis would be strictly a one-off acquisition. But once it was in Ashcroft's possession something of a passion developed, leading to what has become a lifetime's quest to acquire and preserve as many examples as possible of what he describes as the 'tangible relic of an individual's service and bravery – a wonderful tribute to someone who has risked his life for his comrades, his monarch or whatever motivates him in the heat of battle.'

Spanning all three services and nearly 130 years from the Crimean War to the Falklands, Lord Ashcroft's collection will join around fifty VCs already on display at the museum and includes five medals won by First World War air aces and two of the eleven which were awarded after a force of just 150 officers and men fought a famous defensive action against 4,000 Zulus at Rorke's Drift. The new gallery is also very much an Ashcroft initiative, being funded by his donation of £5 million to the museum expressly for this purpose.

Sadly, so far at least, neither his collection nor the museum's include a VC and Bar, the award of a second medal having been made only three occasions in more than a century and a half. Interestingly, two of the three involved were officers of the Royal Army Medical Corps – formerly billeted on Millbank – the medics enjoying the not inconsiderable distinction of being the third most successful military unit in terms of the number of VCs awarded.

Of the three, Lt-Col. Arthur Martin-Leake (1874–1953) is perhaps the most interesting in that his valour was recognised during two different wars. Martin-Leake received his first VC in the Boer War, a bar being added to this during the First World War for which he had volunteered being too old for conscription. The second hero, Captain Noel Godfrey Chavasse (1884–1917) died of wounds sustained at Ypres, but not before he had been transported away from the front by the 46th Field Ambulance, Col. Martin-Leake's own unit. Even more extraordinary, perhaps, is the fact that the third of the double-VCs, Captain Charles Upham who died in 1994 aged 86, was related by marriage to the late Captain Chavasse.

What were **Hitler's plans** for London, if he **won**?

In 1925 a Scottish confidence trickster famously managed to sell Nelson's Column to an unknowing American for

£6,000 – apparently Arthur Furguson also found takers for Buckingham Palace and for Big Ben, although he got only a grand for the latter. But in 1940, when Hitler decided he wanted it, he clearly had no intention of handing over so much as a *pfennig* for the pleasure.

In fact the Nazis had their eye on several monuments scattered around London, the Führer hoping first to ship Nelson back to Berlin following the successful prosecution of *Unternehmen Seelöwe* – otherwise known as Operation Sealion – his plan to invade Britain once he had secured his position across the Channel in France.

We know this because of an SS minute dated 26 August 1940 in which an official assigned to 'Department III' notes that, 'there is no symbol of British Victory in the World War corresponding to the French monument at Compiègne . . . On the other hand, ever since the Battle of Trafalgar, the Nelson Column represents for England a symbol of British Naval might and world domination. It would be an impressive way of underlining the German victory if the Nelson Column were to be transferred to Berlin.'

Cleopatra's Needle (q.v.) was on his shopping list too, though for less obvious reasons, while a series of maps and aerial photographs unearthed by an historian in Germany in 2008 – and the fact that the Luftwaffe generally steered clear of Blackpool, despite it being a major centre of bomber production for the RAF – would seem to suggest that the German top brass fancied transforming the popular Lancashire seaside resort into some kind of Nazi holiday camp if and when they won the war.

Back in the capital another highly prominent landmark to escape the attentions of the enemy was the University of London's Senate House, German bomber crews failing to hit the immensely tall, immensely white, immensely obvious building apparently only because they had been warned off doing so as Hitler wished to use it as his northern European HQ. (Ironically, for a building whose design in recent years has been written off as 'Stalinist', the British fascist leader Oswald Mosley also took a shine to the university's administrative block, declaring in the 1930s that he planned to use it to house parliament in the unlikely event of his ever taking power.)

Similarly, while there was never any suggestion that the masters of the 1,000-year Reich would quit Berlin permanently, Hitler once boasted that by August 1940 he would be in Buckingham Palace, waving from the famous balcony. Happily 'the Few' intervened, winning air superiority during the Battle of Britain and ensuring that by 17 September 1940 – just three weeks after that hubristic Department III memo – Operation Sealion was postponed indefinitely.

What would have happened to **no. 10** had the **Cold War** warmed up?

In 1937 no. 10 Downing Street was comfortable enough but hardly secure from attack and so work began on a secret Cabinet 'citadel' beneath the streets of Dollis Hill. However, deeply reluctant to move so far from the Commons, Winston Churchill refused to use it, preferring to work and sleep in what is now the Churchill Musem and Cabinet War Rooms deep below Storey's Gate.

Despite a 17ft thick layer of protective concrete, however, the likelihood of nuclear war a couple of decades later called for something even more considerable. Accordingly in the 1950s plans were drawn up for an entirely new Central Government War Headquarters – codenamed at various times 'Stockwell', 'Turnstile', 'Subterfuge' and 'Burlington' – which was to be built beneath a 240-acre site many miles from London at Corsham in Wiltshire.

For the most part some 120ft underground, this was to be the hub of the country's entire wartime administration, an alternative seat of power if London was rendered unsafe (or even uninhabitable by a nuclear strike from the countries of the Soviet Eastern Bloc). Carved out from a disused Bath Stone quarry, its true purpose was first revealed by the investigative journalist and *Guardian* columnist Duncan Campbell in the 1980s, having for the previous three decades been taken for nothing more than an ordinary supplies depot.

The complex itself is truly vast, extending well over half a mile below ground level and with more than 60 miles of road above it. It was kitted out to provide living and working accommodation not just for the Prime Minister and his no. 10 staff but also Cabinet members, scores of senior civil servants and Whitehall administrators, and a veritable army of more junior domestic and support staff.

Blast proof and designed to be completely self-sufficient, the facility would have enabled an estimated 4,000 people to live in complete isolation from the world above and to do so safely, if claustrophobically, for up to three months. Fully equipped with a hospital, kitchens, canteens, dormitories, laundries and storerooms, an underground reservoir and treatment plant to provide the water necessary for drinking and washing, it also housed four massive generators and twelve huge fuel tanks to light the tunnels 24 hours a day and maintain the ambient temperature at around 20°C.

Consideration was also given to the BBC, which had its own emergency studio complex at Corsham, although few at the corporation would have known about it at the time. (Many quite senior civil servants would not have known about its existence either, despite having been allocated a desk there for the day when Whitehall finally became 'hot'.)

For all the subterfuge and clever technology, however, the reality is that the entire complex was almost certainly more or less redundant by the time it was completed: the creation of the new Intercontinental Ballistic Missiles (ICBMs) would have seen to that. Nevertheless it remained in operation for more than thirty years, being taken over by the MoD at the end of the Cold War but only finally decommissioned in December 2004 by which time it was home to a skeleton crew of just four.

... And the **royal family**?

While it is abundantly clear from a much later story in the *News of the World* that George VI and Queen Elizabeth were badly shaken up when Buckingham Palace was hit in 1940 ('Queen Mum: Hitler gave me a knee-trembler') the two were determined to stay in London for the duration of the war with Her Majesty famously declaring, 'I'm glad we've been bombed. It makes me feel I can look the East End in the face.'

The queen's courage and political sensitivities notwithstanding, however, the Government would naturally have had to make arrangements in case things turned really ugly. After all, between 1939 and 1945 the Palace was hit a total of seven times, and it seems reasonable to assume that, had that war or the later Cold War gone the wrong way, a means would have had to be found to spirit the family away to safety.

Because of this assumption, rumours abound of secret tunnels radiating out from Buckingham Palace to provide a link to fast routes out of the capital. Of these the first is said to run beneath Green Park to the Piccadilly Line, thereby making for a rapid escape route to Heathrow Airport. A second gives on to the Victoria Line – which runs even closer to the Palace – with another, shorter one connecting with the Guards' Wellington Barracks just over the road.

It has to be said, however, that the evidence for any one of these is scant to say the least, although there is plenty of other subterranean accommodation in the immediate vicinity in which even these most important VIPs could perhaps have taken refuge. The aforementioned Storey's Gate complex, for example, of which the Cabinet War Rooms form only a tiny proportion, is only a few hundred metres from the Palace and with a total of 200 underground offices extends to more than 6 acres.

Even closer, at other end of the Mall, is the former Admiralty Citadel, an immense ivy-clad block complete with pillbox defences and hugely thick blast-proof walls of compressed pebble and flint blocks. Churchill memorably described it as that 'vast monstrosity which weighs upon the Horse Guards Parade' but in his memoirs he recognised its considerable value in terms of propaganda and morale-building, admitting 'it was good to feel we had [it] under our lee.'

He wasn't wrong, either. Like an architectural iceberg the Admiralty's blockhouse extends at least as far underground as it does above it, and was described after the war by Naval Intelligence expert Donald McLachlan as 'probably the best bomb-proof headquarters in London'. Given all that, it would have provided a far more sensible short-term refuge for the royal family than a trip to Heathrow – particularly if there is any truth in yet another rumour of a fourth (or is it fifth?) tunnel running the length of the Mall and which is said to be accessible through a large vent in a door of the gents' loos at the neighbouring ICA. . . .